To Ronnie

With a

Allen

WITH A FOREWORD BY **ROBERT A. G. MONKS**

Capitalism *for* Tomorrow

REUNITING OWNERSHIP AND CONTROL

Allen Sykes

CAPSTONE

Copyright © Allen Sykes 2000

The right of Allen Sykes to be identified as the author of this work has been asserted in accordance with the Copyright, Designs and Patents Act 1988

First published 2000 by

Capstone Publishing Ltd
8 Newtec Place
Magdalen Road
Oxford OX4 1RE
United Kingdom
http://www.capstone.co.uk

British Library Cataloguing in Publication Data
A CIP catalogue record for this book is available from the British Library

ISBN 1-84112-107-X

Typeset by
Forewords, Oxford
Printed and bound by
T.J. International Ltd, Padstow, Cornwall

This book is printed on acid-free paper

Substantial discounts on bulk quantities of Capstone books are available to corporations, professional associations and other organizations. If you are in the USA or Canada, contact the LPC Group for details (tel: 1-800-626-4330; fax 1-800-243-0138); everywhere else, contact Capstone Publishing (tel: +44-1865-798623; fax: +44-1865-240941).

Contents

III Remedies

Acknowledgements

No book covering a wide range of subjects can be written without considerable help from friends and colleagues. I am indebted to all of them. Over a dozen read the original manuscript and their comments and insights were invaluable, particularly those of John Plender and Alan Gregory. I am particularly indebted to former colleagues at Willis Corroon, to many friends at Schroders, to Fred Bleasdale and Kevin Hains at Francis Townsend for their expert help on pension matters, to the National Association of Pension Funds for answering endless requests for data and articles, and to Professor Chris Hendry of the City Business School for providing a wide selection of books, articles, and research papers to guide me through the minefield of management remuneration and performance. I am grateful to McKinseys and the Centre for Tomorrow's Company for allowing me to quote freely from their many comprehensive publications for a key section of the book. Particular thanks are due to Richard Burton and his colleagues at Capstone for being all that one values in a publisher, and to my son Jeremy for the diagrams. Above all, I am indebted to Robert Monks for innumerable illuminating discussions over the last five years, and for his never-failing encouragement to write this book.

With so much help on so many subjects there are bound to be errors and omissions for which I take sole responsibility, as I do for the judgements expressed.

A very special debt is owed to my ever-resourceful and endlessly patient secretary of many years, Mary Huggins. Finally, I wish to thank my wife, Dorothy, most warmly for her steady encouragement and many sacrifices while this book was researched and written.

Foreword

This is a very brave book. There have been so many writings in this field that any author must overcome scepticism and contribute something genuinely new and useful. Allen Sykes succeeds in a compelling style that is learned, concerned and clear. This is a book about power, about those who exercise it and about those who would like to exercise it. History provides very few examples of people with power who are comfortable giving it up. This reluctance extends to the language of discourse. With so many powerful people and groups protecting privileged positions, there is compelling absence of clarity in looking at corporate governance from the perspective of the public good. Allen Sykes combines a wide experience, great intellectual courage in challenging established sacred cows, and the ability to write with the voice of an experienced international businessman, all to the benefit of the interested reader and citizen.

This is a difficult field, because it requires the use of language from several proud disciplines – law, economics, management ethics – and the harmonizing of secular concepts. Aside from the intrinsic linguistic difficulty, one is forced to acknowledge that many honourable and intelligent people solemnly elicit concepts and use words knowing that they are being misleading. For example, the 'First Commandment of Corporate Governance' is that company directors are elected by the members. It is perfectly clear that this is not so and that the members' participation in the process of directoral election might more properly be called coerced ratification. Everyone takes comfort in the supposed duty of independent auditors to shareholders and yet a couple of years ago the Employer's Union proposed not to place the question of auditor selection before the Annual General Meeting. This had the brief benefit of calling attention to the tenuous nature of the auditor's legal obligations to shareholders. People talk about shareholders; they talk of there being contradictory duties owed to shareholders and to so-called stakeholders. Who are these shareholders? Are they arbitrageurs? Are they computer traders holding positions for a nanosecond? Are they pension funds with a holding period over seven years, or are they index funds that are virtually perpetual owners? Nobody seems to process the obvious fact that the duty owed to each of these different classes of shareholders is incompatible with the duty owed to the other classes. No fiduciary can be meaningfully responsible to a class of beneficiaries when different constituents have not only different, but mutually inconsistent interests. The notion of corporate stakeholders is beguiling, but what does it mean? Are there obligations to employees beyond those settled at the bargaining table and the further entitlements available due to their status as the largest class of beneficial owners of corporations? What is owed to suppliers beyond reputable business practice? Companies survive only if they have satisfied customers – what further obligation arises out of the nomenclature that includes them as 'stakeholders'. Finally, how can we talk meaningfully about activist shareholders when, with very few, very brave exceptions – CREF in the United States, Hermes in the United Kingdom – none of the private company pension funds or their money managers are involved. How can we understand a field when so much of the conventional wisdom is so plainly misleading and contradictory?

If one were to read only one book on corporate governance it should be this one. Uniquely, it demonstrates that passive, absentee ownership is the fundamental weakness undermining the full efficiency and accountability of Anglo-American capitalism. The book performs the unique service of providing original, practicable and integrated remedies to this and other weaknesses to the clear benefit of shareholders, managements, employees and pension fund members alike. What is special about this book is that it reflects the wide experience of the author in the world of international business, of large ventures, of coping with governance in many different countries and of understanding what it is that makes business work.

From the perspective of an American, Allen Sykes has all the virtues that we are wont to ascribe to Englishmen. He is plain spoken, he is widely educated, he has vast experience, he fears no man and he speaks the truth. This is an important book, it sets a standard not achieved by any of its predecessors in the considerable literature of corporate governance.

Robert A. G. Monks

**"The vote is worth little without the institutions
to make it continuously effective"**

de Tocqueville

Introduction

The subject of this book is the wider governance aspect of British capitalism today, and why, despite high economic success and employment, there is nevertheless widespread dissatisfaction with our version of capitalism. It is also about what our capitalism could be tomorrow if present problems and weaknesses can be addressed. It is a businessman's contribution to the perennially important debate on economic and corporate governance, on how best to ensure a humane, confident, efficient and globally competitive society which commands the allegiance of its citizens.

There have been a plethora of investigatory reports, articles and books on economic and corporate governance in Britain in the last decade, but the significant weaknesses, well identified by 1990, are largely intact. The only justification for another governance book is to show that the weaknesses are more complex, extensive, damaging and mutually reinforcing than has been generally appreciated, and that they can be overcome. They will yield only to much more relevant, comprehensive and practicable remedies than those put forward to date.

There are a number of serious weaknesses resulting from the way our governance system has evolved from the earlier system of proprietor capitalism. They are not the fault of any one entity but comprise a *systemic* fault. None can overcome these weaknesses alone – only a co-operative effort can succeed. The main weaknesses comprise: absentee ownership, and the consequent lack of exchange of key information and strategic views between owners and managements, and thus of knowledgeable, reliable support for long-term plans; largely unaccountable managements and fiduciaries; insufficiently independent non-executive directors; often excessive management remuneration poorly linked to long-term performance; too many poor-value takeovers and mergers; unsatisfactory fund management contracts of uncertain duration reinforcing short-termism; widespread conflicts of interest for the main governance players; too many under-trained and alienated employees lacking decent value, mobile pensions; and effectively disenfranchised beneficial shareholders, mainly employees investing for retirement. Taken together, these compounding weaknesses comprise a significant handicap to corporate and thus economic performance and much impair market efficiency.

British capitalism, however, is not falling down, and this book is not part of the all too pervasive declinist literature. Rather, despite the undeniable successes of the last twenty years, British capitalism is falling well short of its achievable potential. Good as we are and have been, we have the possibility of doing better still for all our citizens if we take a fresh look at how the governance aspects of our market system works, and at some of its remediable weaknesses. We have a market economy of which, compared to twenty years ago, we can be rightly proud. But to fulfil its potential it is necessary to eliminate the major conflicts of interest which handicap decision taking. Market capitalism cannot fulfil the requirement of being efficient at allocating resources if, as Stanley Wright put it,[1] shareholders accept *de facto* disenfranchisement of their powers, and leave them almost wholly to senior managements with often conflicting interests.

It is a fundamental tenet of free-market capitalism that the system rests on the effective ownership of private property. It is, therefore, particularly unsatisfactory that by far the largest single category of property, namely stocks and shares, should lack effective ownership. Shareholders have become traders of shares rather than owners of companies. That can and does hand undue power to corporate managements and creates damaging conflicts of interest. We should always heed Adam Smith's warning that 'the directors of joint stock companies being the managers rather of other people's money than of their own, it cannot well be expected that they should watch over it with the same anxious vigilance with which partners in a private copartnery frequently watch over their own'. The equivalent contemporary observation is Milton Friedman's that no one looks after anyone else's property as carefully as his own. And, lest it be thought I am adopting a critical attitude towards others, I write as much about myself, having spent my whole career in business management. It is important that we should try to eliminate the major conflicts of interest in contemporary governance. Unresolved they will undermine respect for the market capitalism which alone can ensure general prosperity. Therefore this book is concerned with practical solutions to overcoming ownership which is neither knowledgeable nor committed, and self-perpetuating boards of directors who are not usually effectively accountable to anyone save in a crisis.

The book is also concerned to show that the alignment of interests, risks and rewards of owners, managements and employees is both desirable and achievable. Much of the contemporary debate on whether companies should be run for their shareholders or stakeholders is misplaced. The fortunes of the two groups are inextricably linked as companies enjoying long-term success have always known and demonstrated. Accordingly, wise managements take into account the long-term interests of all the other groups of participants: their co-operation is integral to corporate success. Further, there is more to the values of the *real* shareholders, the 20 per cent individual shareholders and the 80 per cent of collective beneficial shareholders (pension fund members, insurance policyholders, etc.) than 'shareholder value', particularly the short-term variant of it. The governance debate has been unproductively narrowed by such an approach.

The theme running through the book is that while there are many important and mutually reinforcing governance weaknesses, the fundamental weakness is passive absentee ownership. Only if it is effectively remedied can all the other weaknesses be resolved. Owners look after their property better than third parties, but shareholders, particularly the 80 per cent of beneficial shareholders, are not in a position to look after their shareholdings properly to reflect fully their own values and long-term interests. The present investment intermediaries are prevented by disabling conflicts of interest from serving their interests in a fully effective way, and in particular both to hold corporate managements fully accountable and, equally importantly, to support optimal longer-term strategies. As a result neither companies nor the economy achieve their full potential. Beneficiaries, employees, etc., pay the price. A way has to be found to break the deadlock. This book suggests how this might best be effected by a combination of modest catalytic government actions and the freeing of market forces to deliver a superior result and a more cohesive society.

The starting point is to observe that there can be no generally successful system of corporate governance for Britain, i.e. one that produces a humane, confident, efficient and globally competitive society, without at least three *interdependent* preconditions:

- sufficient committed, knowledgeable and active long-term shareholders;
- managements with the preconditions and incentives for long-term performance who are accountable to such shareholders; and
- motivated and valued employees and stakeholders.

I hope to show how these preconditions could be achieved in the belief that others who share the sense of this approach can and will improve upon it.

Dedication
To individual and beneficial shareholders everywhere

Executive Summary

The double deficit

The essence of any system of governance is that those to whom major powers are entrusted must be accountable to those whom they serve. British corporate governance fails this test. The accountability that exists is typically limited and delayed. Managements are not effectively accountable either to individual shareholders (20 per cent) or to the investment institutions and fund managers, etc. (80 per cent), who are the intermediary agents of the ultimate shareholders. Nor, in turn, are these intermediaries effectively accountable to the ultimate share-holders, the individuals who are pension fund members, policyholders, etc. There is thus a double accountability deficit.

The legal fiction

The legal intent of corporate governance is that shareholders appoint directors, in particular non-executive directors, who are sufficiently independent to hold executive directors fully and satisfactorily accountable. They also appoint the auditors to report on directors' stewardship of companies. This view is summarized in Figure 1.

The reality

The reality is very different. With the pervasiveness of largely absentee

Figure 1 Shareholder control – the legal fiction
Companies and their managements accountable to shareholders

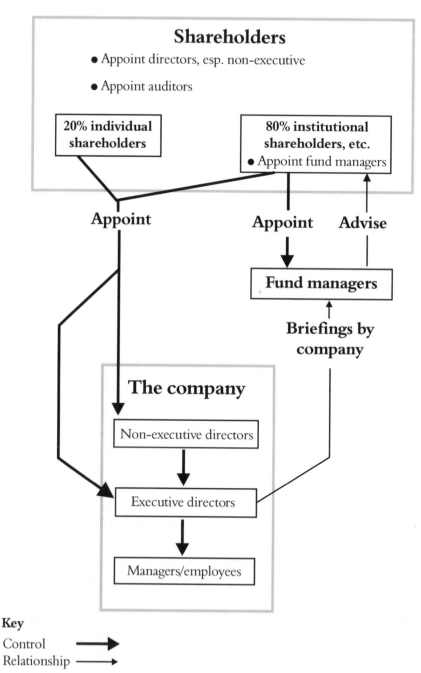

Key

Control ⟶

Relationship ⟶

ownership, managements are essentially self-governing and self-perpetuating. Most governance power has passed to executive directors, particularly chairman and chief executive officers. The latter effectively choose the non-executive directors, largely from their peers in other companies ('the monitored choose the monitors'), who thus lack full independence. They also choose the auditors, the consultants for the executive remuneration committees, and the fund managers for the corporate pension schemes which now own over a quarter of all equities. This represents an unprecedented concentration of corporate governance power in the hands of the very few, with the top 100 companies representing 77 per cent of the value of all quoted companies. Inescapably this concentration of power has led to widely recognized abuses by executive directors, to often huge remuneration packages poorly related to performance, and to takeovers and mergers frequently driven by managements' motives rather than shareholders' interests. The remuneration of managements, in large part by share options, is a one-way bet allowing them to share in shareholder success at no financial risk. All this is not efficient free market capitalism. If owners are not fully in charge of their assets, then the market cannot fulfil its prime requirement of allocating resources efficiently in everyone's interests.

Shareholders in aggregate still possess the latent powers to hold corporate managements accountable, but save in rare crisis or scandal these powers are seldom deployed. They have been neutered by the growth of institutional shareholders (and equivalent) to the point at which these own nearly 80 per cent of all shares and who, with the fund managers, are subject to serious conflicts of interest which seriously hinder their effectiveness in holding management accountable. Given that virtually all institutions and fund managers have widely spread portfolios to minimize risk, individual holdings in any large quoted company are consequently small. This makes active individual exercise of shareholder control uneconomic (the 'free-rider' problem), and collective action between competing entities infrequent. Corporate pension fund trustees (25 per cent) are discouraged from taking active governance roles by their own managements who benefit from general shareholder passivity. Insurance companies (25 per cent) usually have their own fund managers who compete with independent fund managers for the highly profitable major corporate pension fund business.

They are generally disinclined to hold managements accountable where this might threaten the retention of existing accounts and the seeking of new ones. Both groups have a vested interest in seldom closely questioning directors' remuneration, etc., lest the same critical scrutiny fall on their own directors. The result is largely absentee ownership with managements exercising powers in default that properly belong to owners.

The real shareholders

While the investment institutions, etc., are the major (80 per cent) shareholders in quoted companies, in fact they are the intermediary agents of the many millions of pension fund members, policyholders, unit trust holders, etc. These beneficiaries are the majority of the ultimate real shareholders whose interests must always be properly considered. But as the investment intermediaries have no effective contact with them, there is little accountability. There are thus two major and reinforcing accountability or democratic deficits. Corporate managements are not effectively accountable to the investment institutions, nor the investment institutions to the ultimate shareholders.

The systemic fault

All this is not a criticism of corporate managements who have necessarily assumed powers relinquished by shareholders. Indeed it is not anyone's fault. Rather it is the consequence of the way the governance system has slowly evolved over many decades with the decline of powerful controlling shareholders. In sum, there is a *systemic* fault. Nearly all the main governance weaknesses are the consequences of this fault, and in particular passive ownership and thus largely unaccountable managements. This analysis is summarized in Figure 2. It has resulted in a corporate governance system in which executive directors, and particularly chairmen and CEOs, are implicitly, in Robert Monks's memorable phrase 'trustees for the public good'. Given the major conflicts of interest this is a quite inappropriate responsibility, but it is the inescapable consequence of the systemic fault.

Figure 2 Shareholder control – the contemporary reality

Largely passive shareholders and unaccountable managements – executive directors
implicitly 'trustees for the public good'

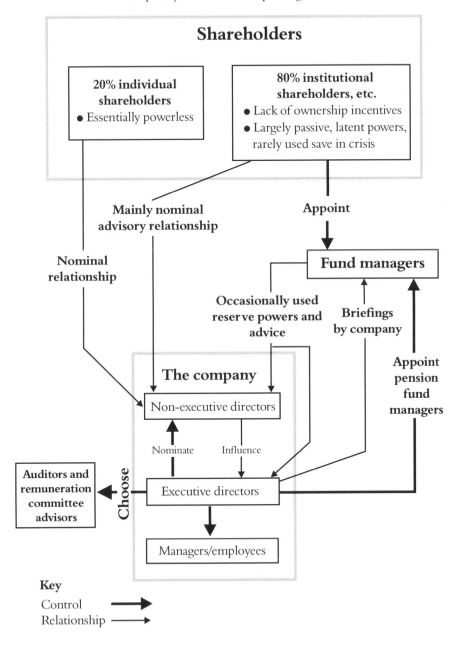

Shareholders vs. stakeholders – a false dilemma

The resolution of the identified serious governance weaknesses first requires agreement on a major current concern, whether companies are to be run solely or mainly in the shareholders' interests or whether interests of employees and other stakeholder groups should be included.[1] On the basis that 'shareholder' interests means the 20 per cent direct individual shareholders and the 80 per cent indirect beneficial shareholders – who together comprise the real shareholders – then, within the law, shareholder primacy must prevail. Any wider objective would be unworkable. For centuries, however, successive governments have introduced laws to protect employees, to guarantee rights to join trade unions, to provide for redundancy, etc., and to protect consumers, the environment, etc., a process that will continue. All companies are bound by these laws. But there is strong evidence to show that companies which go beyond their strict legal liabilities and take reasonable account of employee and other stakeholders' interests thereby enhance shareholder value. This is because shareholder interests are best met by also taking account of the *general* long-term interests of all the stakeholders on whom corporate success depends: it is a *joint* product. All companies with sustained long-term performance work on these principles. That said, particular and short-term stakeholder interests must often be sacrificed for the greater general good. The wider groups cannot long prosper if shareholders languish – the company would eventually cease to exist. But hard choices are inescapable. To survive and prosper all companies must be prepared to adjust all inputs when necessary (staff reductions, changing suppliers, ceasing to supply some customers, relocating production, etc.), hence the undesirability of stakeholder board representatives. But when it is remembered that the real ultimate shareholders are largely the same people as the stakeholders, there is no fundamental long-term conflict of interests between the two groups. This is particularly so bearing in mind that the ultimate prime need for stakeholders is decent pensions, which depend overwhelmingly on stock market performance. Hence the general primacy of shareholder interests, realistically viewed, is clearly in stakeholders' general long-term interest.

The value of good governance

A further important consideration affecting governance improvements is to take note of the strong evidence – provided notably by McKinsey but also by others – that well-governed companies – i.e. those with fully accountable directors and those with effective owners – deliver significant benefits for both shareholders and all other stakeholders. Such companies largely avoid management abuses which are a prime cause of the discrediting of Anglo-American market capitalism. Given the hugely successful results of such capitalism in raising living standards, the elimination of the causes of such seriously detrimental criticism should be a shared objective of business, government and the main political parties.

Well-governed companies are also more likely to avoid persisting in failing policies and strategies with their attendant economic losses, which are often the cause of unnecessary hardship to employees, suppliers, communities, etc. Such companies are also more likely to perform better in the long term and thus deliver superior shareholder value as well as better job security and pensions for their employees. In part this is because such companies are judged by the stock market to be less risky, not only because they are less prone to mistakes, but also because well-governed companies generally correct mistakes more quickly.

A prime example of the value of good governance is Warren Buffett's investment firm, Berkshire-Hathaway, which has been brilliantly successful for over thirty years. The company takes large, long-term, even very long-term stakes in a handful of companies, usually on highly preferential terms, and a seat on the board. These developments are widely welcomed by the other investors and corporate managements concerned because Berkshire-Hathaway's involvement has nearly always greatly enhanced shareholder value. It would be wrong to attribute Berkshire-Hathaway's success mainly to good long-term corporate governance. The legendary investment vision of Warren Buffett is the prime cause, but he has always been America's strongest advocate of the significant value attributable to good governance combined with long-term investment, i.e. active, knowledgeable, committed ownership.

In sum, the provision of a good corporate governance system, one that provides for full accountability, adds to economic wealth.

Achieving reform

The acceptance, even the widespread acceptance of this analysis of the contemporary corporate governance *malaise* would be very unlikely to lead any of the main participants to change the status quo. Corporate managements are unlikely voluntarily to relinquish their extensive powers. The investment institutions and fund managers, who largely compete among themselves, lack the means and incentives to overcome their entrenched and paralysing conflicts of interest. The real shareholders, the majority ultimate beneficiaries and the minority individual shareholders, are effectively voiceless. Effective change can come only from government action. Fortunately, three catalytic but modest government actions could break the deadlock by giving all parties the incentives to provide or procure changes which would overcome the weaknesses, the double accountability deficit. Market forces would then be freed to do the rest.

Catalytic government actions

The need is for a programme of initially minimal reform which addresses the identified double accountability deficit in corporate governance in an efficient and practicable way. Given the complexity and importance of the issues, and the difficulty of seeing how reforms would work out in practice, reform should be evolutionary and directed towards encouraging investment institutions and fund managers to evolve their own solutions within the framework of the essential reforms now being proposed. The process would require a corporate governance regulator, one of whose responsibilities would be to review reform progress after three years to determine whether or not the initial reforms needed to be strengthened or modified.

The first requirement, desirably with cross-party agreement, is that the government should affirm that creating an effective shareholder presence in all companies is in the national interest, that there should be no power without accountability, and that this principle should be taken into account by all regulators, the takeover panel, the competition authority, etc. With the direct and indirect ownership of equities being, with housing, the largest personal assets by far, nothing less than effective accountability should be politically acceptable to any of the main political parties.

The second requirement is that all pension fund trustees and other fiduciaries holding shares, must act *solely* in the long-term interests of their beneficiaries and for the *exclusive* purpose of providing them with benefits. (While it can fairly be argued that this is already trust law, it needs to be given specific, continuous and strong public emphasis and enforcement to overcome present inertia and conflicts of interest – i.e. to make trustees, fiduciaries, etc., proactive in the sole and exclusive interest of their beneficiaries.)

The third requirement, to give full effect to the first two proposals, is that the institutional shareholders should be made accountable for exercising their votes in an informed and sensible manner above some sensibly determined minimum holding (e.g. £10m). As votes are an asset (voting shares always have a market premium over non-voting ones) they should be used to further beneficiaries' interests on all occasions. In effect, the voting of all institutionally held shares would be virtually compulsory.

All three proposals are both necessary and mutually reinforcing. To be compelled to vote without, say, the requirement to do so solely and exclusively in the interests of beneficiaries would be likely, given the inescapably continuing conflicts of interest, to result in institutions taking the line of least resistance. There would be, as at present, an almost automatic vote in support of nearly all corporate management proposals. It would thus give the spurious appearance of democratic accountability while leaving the reality of the double accountability deficit intact.

The purpose of the three proposed government actions is to make both corporate managements and investment institutions effectively accountable to the ultimate shareholders, the millions of beneficiaries who comprise the majority of the working population. They could not, of course, be directly answerable to this huge number of individuals, each with small, individually held beneficial interests in a myriad of companies. The three measures are designed, however, to ensure that trustees and fiduciaries have both the necessity and means to respond *solely and exclusively to their beneficiaries' collective long-term interests.*

An outline programme for reform

Inadequate corporate and institutional accountability is seen to impair efficiency and hence national wealth creation. It also results in the abuse of management remuneration, etc., thus harming the public acceptance of free markets essential to maximum economic growth.

The following proposals which address these issues should form the substance of a government Green Paper for public discussion with the intent of introducing a flexible and effective system for ensuring adequate accountability for UK-based companies. (Overseas companies pose special problems which could only effectively be addressed by co-operation between governments.)

1. *Widening the regulatory remit*   The existing regulator, the Financial Services Authority, whose remit already covers standards of probity and competence for financial institutions, should have its remit extended to cover the exercise of due diligence by all investment intermediaries in the exercise of their voting rights of all the shares which they hold in UK-based companies either on behalf of third parties or their own shareholders. It is inherently paradoxical that such intermediaries should be tightly regulated as to their honesty and competence in dealing with their investments but under no practical obligation to ensure that shareholder rights in the companies in which they invest are actively, efficiently and continuously discharged, solely and exclusively on behalf of the beneficiaries.

2. *Code of conduct*   The regulatory authority, whether itself, or by establishing a special corporate governance regulator (or 'Ombudsman'), should ensure that the investment institutions would operate within a code of conduct for, say, initially the top 200 companies. The investment institutions should be charged with the following requirements.

- *Due diligence obligations*   To exercise the obligations of due diligence in the discharge of their governance responsibilities in a demonstrably informed, impartial and responsible manner, solely and exclusively in beneficiaries' interest. (This automatically requires them to exercise voting rights on all occasions since not to do so would be a clear violation of such diligence.) Where the due diligence obligation cannot be effectively discharged directly due to conflicts of interest (a very common case) the obligation would be to procure the exercise of those rights by competent investment intermediaries with no conflicts of interest.

- *Ensuring independent non-executive directors*   To ensure that all non-executive directors would be independently selected and nominated. (On an initial trial basis existing non-executive directors could act via a nomination committee – a most sensible Cadbury Report proposal – of which they alone were members. They would also need to be advised by an executive search firm of their own choosing, with no other connections to the company.)

- *Monitoring non-executive directors*   To monitor non-executive directors' activities on the audit, remuneration and nomination committees to ensure they were advised by independent consultants of their own choosing with no other connections to the company or its management. (Thus auditors, whom the audit committee would recommend for annual election to shareholders in place of but after consultation with management, would not also be able to act in the usually far larger role of consultants, because of obvious conflicts of interest, thus ensuring auditors were indisputably fully independent.)

3. *Method of operating*   The corporate governance regulator, in the interests of flexibility and the avoidance of bureaucracy, would work primarily by exception. Using the massive amount of research produced by brokers, independent analysts, the press, etc., the first step would be to identify companies with a history of under-performance or apparent management abuse. Then the major institutional shareholders in these companies would be required to show that they had properly exercised due diligence towards these companies to avoid the apparent failures in corporate accountability in maintaining a high standard of efficiency and probity in matters of remuneration, etc. Where failure to exercise such diligence was apparent, the regulator would request the institutional shareholders to come forward with a programme to remedy these defects forthwith. In cases where the intermediary investors had

conspicuously failed in this respect, the regulator would have the power to 'name and shame'. It is for consideration whether there should also be the power to fine the investors, a matter which could be considered by the regulator in the first or a subsequent three-year review.

Achieving effective accountability

Such a system of regulation would not instantly rectify all the identified defects of accountability. But there is every chance that over time, and applied apolitically, the market forces of competition between investing institutions and the concern to avoid being 'named and shamed', as well as the provision of positive measures (the common obligation on all such investors to perform due diligence ensuring collective action) would bring about major improvements.

The simple obligation of due diligence in exercising voting rights is of far-reaching consequence. First there would be the sanction of adverse publicity for investment institutions failing to discharge their obligations. Second, the regulator could additionally recommend significant fines. Lastly, the institutions would be open to legal action by beneficiaries for any significant loss suffered as the result of continued negligence.

These actions, taken together, would go a long way towards effect-ively enfranchising beneficial shareholders and eliminating the double accountability deficit, particularly when reinforced by the consequential reactions of markets.

Finally, as individual shareholders are essentially voiceless, it should be considered whether they should have the additional right to elect one non-executive director. As it would be difficult to withdraw such a right, the sensible course might be for interested parties to make representations on the matter to the regulator at the first three-year review.

Possible market responses

The double accountability deficit can be remedied only by government action. The three proposed catalytic government actions as enshrined in the outline programme for reform would put investment institutions, fund managers, etc., under the clear legal obligation to hold corporate managements fully accountable to the interests of the ultimate shareholders. The institutions would have to respond to such obligations. How they would respond in these circumstances would be a matter for individual decisions and the effect of market forces in the changed legal circumstances.

The institutions, certainly the very large insurance companies, could be emboldened henceforth to act directly in the ultimate shareholders' interests on a continuous basis – as a few indeed now do on an occasional selective basis. If they were seen to be able to discharge their new responsibilities effectively, other institutions could follow their example, including perhaps some of the large corporate pension funds. The same could apply to some of the large fund managers where the investment institutions delegate their governance obligations. For the majority of investment institutions, however, the continuing serious conflicts of interest would lead them to delegate their obligations to competent new specialist intermediaries which market forces would cause to emerge. In the interests of evaluating the efficacy of the proposed government actions some possible market responses are considered next. It must be stressed, however, that other and perhaps superior market responses could emerge. Indeed, as the investment institutions and regulators feel their way, it is likely that continually improving market responses would result.

Special Purpose Trust Companies

The most likely initial development to meet the needs of the majority of investment institutions seeking to delegate their corporate governance obligations would be the emergence of a new form of investment intermediary performing such services for a fee since no suitable entity presently exists. Robert Monks has proposed just such a service company which he has termed a 'Special Purpose Trust Company' (SPTC). The sole function of these newly formed independent institutions would be to act as owner with respect to voting the shares held in the investment portfolios of its institutional clients – i.e. to exercise independent judgement in voting their clients' shares. To discharge this function they would have to be completely independent institutions with no commercial relationships with the companies to which their clients' shares related. Staff would need a background in corporate governance and accountability. In practice, many would have a legal, accounting, financial or business background. However, the staff would not be managing businesses nor would they ever hold non-executive directorships. Their primary concern would be to create standards to guide corporate managers and by which they would be judged. As they must have no conflicts of interest, the best form of organization would be a professional partnership, i.e. controlled and owned by their principals. Further, senior staff should not be there only temporarily before resuming a business career because of the obvious conflicts of interest. Hence senior posts should be held only for the last, say, 5–10 years before retirement.

SPTCs would be paid fees for their services to institutional clients, determined competitively. The first responsibility of SPTCs would be to monitor managements, vote on the appointments of all directors and ultimately vote to change boards if required. As long as the nomination committees of non-executive directors put forward competent and independent candidates for non-executive director vacancies, SPTCs would not need to find candidates themselves. But if in too many companies some unsuitable candidates were nominated, then the SPTCs, acting collectively, would need to form one or more organizations, supported by independent executive search firms, to find and recommend suitable independent candidates. (Such candidates would need to be predominantly businesspeople to carry the support of direct and institutional shareholders, SPTCs and corporate managements.) The second responsibility would be to provide guidance to managements on the long-term needs of owners, e.g. long-term remuneration incentives properly linked to performance, and requiring executive directors to share appropriately in investors' risks, perhaps by purchasing and *holding* a significant shareholding.

It is important to note that SPTCs would represent *a competitive market solution* to corporate governance needs. Their fees, and indeed their very existence, would depend on offering a valued commercial service in full competition with other providers.

The emergence of SPTCs in combination with the new corporate governance legal obligations and a regulator could well ensure sufficient accountability by both corporate managements and investment institutions such that no further developments would be needed. If, however, it became apparent that the combined direct action by some of the large institutions and SPTCs were unable to hold managements satisfactorily accountable, other types of institutions would be required, or might anyway emerge because of the extra benefits they could offer investment institutions in addition to taking over their legal obligation to act solely and exclusively in beneficiaries' interests. Two forms of intermediaries might emerge, 'specialist investors' and 'relationship investors', both based on the benefits from small concentrated specialist investment portfolios holding shares for the longer term and seeking board representation. The model for such entities would be Warren Buffett's Berkshire-Hathaway company previously described.

Specialist investors

'Specialist Investors' (SIs) would in effect be specialist investment trusts aiming to hold 4–5 per cent shareholdings in perhaps only 5–10 companies. They would have small but experienced staffs made up of successful business executives and investment analysts. Their function would be to select a very small number of companies for long-term investment and to be able and willing to act as supportive and knowledgeable long-term owners. In support of that activity they would seek board representation. (If competent, SPTCs and institutions would be likely to support their candidate directors. And, unlike SPTCs, the senior members of the SIs could and should be independent non-executive directors in the companies in which they invested, there being no conflicts of interests.) Their shareholders would be mainly the investment institutions who would thus be relieved of corporate governance obligations in the underlying shares, although not for their shareholdings in the SIs. Such investor companies would offer investment institutions a potentially attractive way of securing the Berkshire-Hathaway type benefits of active, knowledgeable and committed share ownership in major companies. As with SPTCs, SIs would have to compete for business, hence they too would represent a competitive market solution for responsible share investment.

Relationship investors

The major investment institutions tend to hold investments in a large number of the top 200 companies for eight years or more on average, although they often trade actively in a part of such shareholdings. As no actual commitment to long-term holding is made, the Berkshire-Hathaway type advantages which accrue from an active, committed, stable relationship are foregone by investors and corporate managements alike. In addition to SIs, these advantages could be achieved by investment institutions and fund managers putting a proportion of their major company shareholdings in 'relationship investors' (RIs). Each RI would seek, on a very small portfolio of shares of perhaps 5–10 companies, to hold, say, 2 per cent of mega companies and up to 4 or 5 per cent of the rest of the top 100/200 companies, i.e. enough for influence but not dominance, typically holding shares for five years or more. They would each nominate suitable businesspeople to be independent, non-executive directors ('shareholder directors') voted on by all shareholders, and each backed up by a small secretariat to put them on equal terms with their executive colleagues. Their duties would, as now, be to *all* shareholders but they would be providing fully independent and well supported director candidates who, if elected, would be able to count on the support of their RI. As most investment institutions and SPTCs, etc., would also tend to support them, they would be in a stronger position to hold corporate managements accountable. Equally, their knowledgeable support for approved longer-term management strategies would also be likely to result in widespread shareholder support, thus giving managements the confidence to undertake such strategies where passive absentee ownership and volatile share prices might otherwise make them too difficult or risky.

RIs and SIs could be paid a slightly enhanced competitively, determined dividend *as decided by all shareholders* to cover their extra costs and responsibilities. This would be a market reward for the service of providing ownership stability and truly independent non-executive directors on equal terms with executive directors and thus more able to hold them fully accountable. It would overcome the free-rider problem and be to the clear benefit of all shareholders and ultimately all stakeholders. RIs could comprise both the larger investment institutions or syndicates of such institutions, probably organized by fund managers for a fee. This system would not tie up institutionally held shares for any longer than at present, and an RI could always sell out before five years by forfeiting the enhanced dividends and another take its place. It would be ideally suited to tracker funds with their very long-term holdings.

Longer fund management contracts

The final matter to be considered under possible market responses to changed corporate governance requirements concerns the length and security of fund management contracts. Most contracts run for 5–6 years, and some for much longer. But a fund manager would become concerned at the prospect of either dismissal or the loss of a large part of the investment fund's responsibilities if its performance for a client, as measured quarterly, were not to be in the median or top quartile over the previous 2–3 years. Inevitably, this causes fund managers to favour shares expected to perform well on a short-term basis, which puts indirect but significant pressure on many corporate managements to pay more attention to short-term results. This, coupled with widely dispersed share portfolios, weakens investor support for otherwise justified longer-term corporate policies. The ultimate beneficial share-holders – primarily individuals saving for retirement – are of course investors who seek the best long-term returns. There are few incentives for fund managers to take as long term a view as either their investment skills justify if only they could rely on longer-term loyalty from their clients, or as may be in the interests of beneficiaries. Yet it is widely acknowledged that investment performance measured over periods much shorter than five years (some would argue for a full economic cycle) are largely invalid. If, however, the investment institutions, in seeking the best performance for their beneficiaries, come to favour the Berkshire-Hathaway type benefits of more committed long-term ownership, with the concomitant much smaller spread of shares that both SIs and RIs would provide, they should also consider the benefits of extending fund management contracts to an expected period of typically five years, subject to safeguards for interim performance. This would be welcomed by fund managements who would be freed to take longer-term views where justified. It would also complement the development of five-year long-term incentive schemes for corporate managements (presently more usually three years), and thus encourage longer-term corporate policies where desirable and justified.

Capitalism for tomorrow

The effects of the proposed governance reforms would result in some investment institutions, almost certainly a small minority, choosing to discharge their obligations by direct action, with the majority seeking to delegate to specialist intermediaries. The types of intermediaries would depend on the market response, but three possible and complementary responses – SPTCs, SIs and RIs – have been considered. Other and perhaps superior ones could well evolve. In the first instance, as the investment institutions and the regulator are feeling their way, the SPTC response would be likely to predominate, and this is illustrated in Figure 3. Indeed, if SPTCs are fully effective in holding corporate managements accountable, then other types of intermediaries may not be needed. The clear benefits of active, knowledgeable and committed ownership of the Berkshire-Hathaway type, however, may well lead to SIs and RIs and similar developments – the market would decide. But by various means the proposed reforms would ensure that all institutionally held shares (up to 80 per cent) would be voted solely and exclusively in beneficiaries' interests, mainly by SPTCs, and by holding managements truly accountable, all the present major corporate governance weaknesses and conflicts of interest would be overcome. The institutions necessary to ensure that shareholder votes would be used on a continuously effective basis on behalf of the real shareholders would be firmly in place.

Managements would be relieved of their present necessarily assumed but inappropriate non-management powers which properly belong to shareholders. They would be freed from the present rising tide of serious and largely justified criticisms which in any case cannot be ignored much longer. They would then be able to concentrate on corporate performance, their prime responsibility. Finally, managements would have both fully legitimized, generous incentives and the preconditions for long-term performance to the direct benefit of beneficiary investors and shareholders, and to the general but indirect benefit of all stakeholders. The greater ensuring long-term profitability

Figure 3 Shareholder control under due diligence – initial result of enabling government actions

Corporate managements effectively accountable to shareholders via proactive fiduciaries and investment intermediaries

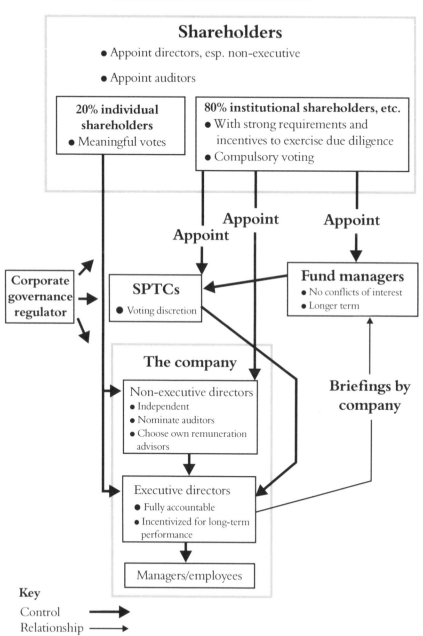

would far outweigh the modest costs of implementation. In sum, all involved would benefit, and all could play to their long-term strengths relieved of conflicts of interest and other handicaps.

The proposed reforms would enable competitive free market forces to perform their prime function, the efficient allocation of resources. As Robert Monks well expressed it, 'Putting owners in charge of what they own is the purest form of capitalism.'

I

Setting the Scene

CHAPTER 1

A Governance Overview of British Capitalism

The declining popularity of business

There is a paradox at the heart of contemporary British capitalism. Britain, jointly with France, is the fourth largest economy in the world. Living standards have never been so high. Unemployment is at its lowest for a generation, prospects for continued economic success are firm, and for the first time this century both the main political parties are in broad agreement on the general superiority of a competitive market-based economic policy. Support for nationalization, protectionism and over-strong trade unions is negligible. Yet public opinion is not supportive of business, the acknowledged engine of growth and prosperity.

The highly regarded polling organization MORI was formed in 1969. It began by assessing public attitudes to the question 'Do you agree that the profits of large British companies help make things better for everyone who buys their goods and services?'[1] Some 53 per cent of respondents agreed, and less than 25 per cent disagreed, a majority of over two to one. When the same question was put nearly thirty years later there were only 25 per cent in favour, and 52 per cent against, a virtual reversing of the earlier result. The downward trend in popularity looks set to continue.

Business popularity peaked in 1980 when a new Conservative government came to power. It began to slide with the 1981–2 recession.

Apart from temporary peaks with Conservative election victories in 1983, 1987 and 1992, the downward trend has continued with the New Labour government having little impact. Business scandals, very high executive remuneration by any past standard, environmental disasters, the perception of a general increase in business ruthlessness, and the decline in perceived job, pension and welfare security have probably all played a part. So too have the growth of hostile takeovers (however necessary) and the fairly widespread and growing unease and distrust, and in some cases fear, amongst a significant proportion of the working population. These developments were persuasively analysed in a recent book by John Plender.[2] They have led to the growth of the stakeholder movement (Chapters 6 and 7) which seeks to put the interests of stakeholders on at least an equal footing with that of shareholders. It led the government in February 1999 to set up a major two-year inquiry, the Company Law Review Steering Group, to advise on the appropriate strategy for modern company law in a competitive economy. The Steering Group has two main tasks: firstly, to decide in whose interests a company should be run; and secondly, how best to ensure that the ultimate values and interests of that group should govern directors' interests. These are the two fundamental issues facing contemporary corporate governance. No longer is there unquestioning acceptance that shareholder interests, nearly entirely comprised of maximizing 'shareholder value', should be the sole or even the main guideline for directors. Shareholder primacy should prevail but unquestioned acceptance of the values of big business is now under serious challenge.

The realization that capitalism needed to re-examine its fundamental tenets, strengths and weaknesses with the demise of Communism led in 1990 to the then editor of *The Economist*, Rupert Pennant-Rea, writing a particularly perceptive article 'Punters or Proprietors'.[3] His main theme concerned the reality, meaning and effectiveness of corporate owner-ship, and the breakdown in corporate governance. As he saw it then, how well firms do depends in large part on the attitudes and behaviour of their owners and staff. He argued that the classical, involved and knowledgeable owner-proprietors of the previous century have largely given way to institutional investors. Personal savings, in part because of tax incentives, but also for convenience and risk sharing, have mainly and irreversibly passed to investment institutions. They lack the interest or the capacity to act as proprietors either singly, or in aggregate. They regard their investments more like betting slips. Shares are bought at hopefully favourable odds to provide winnings which they hope will be large, hedged by numerous other similar bets (investments) on countless other companies. No responsibility is felt for corporate performance, that is for managements. If a share fails to perform it will be sold, or held only until a bid is made for the company.

Owner-capitalists have been largely replaced by 'punter-capitalists' interested in early financial returns. The resultant power vacuum at the heart of corporate governance has been filled, primarily by hostile bidders and partly by aspiring owner-managers (taking companies private). Both want to change the way companies are run and to make money for themselves. Both forces are rejections of punter-capitalism.

The problems, pressures and trends which Pennant-Rea observed are still with us, and few satisfactory remedies have been implemented. Since he wrote we have had the worthy and well-intended reports of Cadbury, Greenbury and Hampel (Chapter 7) which have produced important improvements (particularly Cadbury, which established the permanent importance of good corporate governance). But major disagreements persist between the business establishment, who see little wrong with the market-driven status quo of maximizing shareholder value and those in the stakeholder camp, who believe that the relative neglect of all other relationships is short-sighted, inefficient and divisive. One of the more farsighted of the business community, Paul Myners (chairman of the fund manager, Gartmore, and chairman of the City group which produced a well-regarded report on City/business co-operation[4] commended in the Hampel Report) said, when opening a RSA meeting on American lessons for investor protection on 12 April 1994:

> None of us feel that we have the balance right about the relations between industry, corporate management and those who own the businesses (or stand in place of those who own the businesses), institutional investors.

Few could disagree with that statement, or with one of its consequences, that present corporate governance shortcomings contribute to the decline in business popularity.

Equity returns and prospects

The performance of the stock market is a major influence on corporate governance and all the key players. Equities have been by far the twentieth century's best long-term investment, far exceeding government bonds and treasury bills, and this will continue in the present century. At the end of 1999 we were witnessing a twelve-year bull market, the greatest of the century. This has taken shares, particularly in Britain and America, to unprecedented levels compared with underlying profits. Most experts believe markets may soon suffer a major correction. But no one is forecasting that equities will be displaced as the preferred long-term choice for the provision of retirement funds. The dominance of investment institutions in equity ownership will therefore continue.

The long-term return on equities in the world's leading countries has often been studied. A new, particularly useful and comprehensive study of equity and bond returns, which summarizes the key trends of the entire twentieth century, has just been published by three British academics (Elroy Dimson, Paul Marsh and Mike Saunders) in association with a leading Dutch banking group.[5] It revealed that British equities achieved a real return of 6 per cent over the century rather than the 8 per cent which was the best previous estimate.[6] This breaks down into 4 per cent for 1900–54, and just under 9 per cent for 1955–99. Whether 9 per cent can be maintained over the next ten years or so is strongly questioned by many experts, with 7 per cent being seen as a more likely figure by most, and some believing it will be rather lower.

Companies and their owners

The number of quoted domestic companies, their market capitalization and the value of shares changing hands annually for 1996–9 are shown in Table 1.1

The top 100 companies currently comprise 76.8 per cent of the total market value, and the next 250, the middle size companies (£400–2,700m) would add a further 13.7 per cent (£250m). Thus the top 350 companies comprise just over 90 per cent of total stock market capitalization. Within the top 100 companies, ranging in value from

Table 1.1 UK domestic quoted companies (excluding AIM companies)

	Number of companies end year	End year capitalization (£s bn)		Corrected turnover (value of shares changing hands) (£s bn)
		Total	FTSE 100	
1996	2171	1012	706	371
1997	2157	1252	913	524
1998	2087	1423	1120	623
1999	1945	1820	1398	875

Source: London Stock Exchange.

£2.7bn to over £120bn, the concentration towards a handful of mega companies is also very marked. The top ten companies at the end of 1999 are shown in Table 1.2

At the end of 1999 there were ten international companies larger than any of the top ten in Britain, ranging from Microsoft (£372bn) and General Electric (£313bn) down to Deutsche Telecom (£133bn), and nearly a hundred more as big as the British top ten.

Current prospective mergers and takeovers, if consummated, will alter the British rankings and concentration considerably. The Vodafone–Mannesman mega merger has created a company worth in excess of £225bn, making it the fourth or fifth largest company in the world. The BP Amoco takeover of Arco is worth £130bn, and the proposed SmithKline Beecham and Glaxo Wellcome merger could be worth £95bn. This would mean that the three largest British companies between them could be worth around £450bn, or over 30 per cent of the total UK market capitalization, and the top ten companies over 45 per cent. Such concentration of values in such a small number of companies has occurred before at the turn of the century, in 1929 and in the late 1950s and early 1970s, but it is certainly the highest concentration for twenty-five years.

The annual net turnover of British shares (half of purchases plus sales), i.e. the value of shares changing hands, has been growing steadily over the last four years (Table 1.1). Taking the average of the market capitalization at the beginning and end of the years, the rate of share turnover was about 2.16 in both 1997 and 1998, accelerating to 1.85

Table 1.2 Largest British companies by market capitalization

	Company	Business sector	End 1999 value (£s bn)	Percentage of total value
1	BP Amoco	oil	121.3	6.7
2	British Telecom	telecommunications	98.4	5.4
3	Vodafone AirTouch	telecommunications	95.4	5.2
4	HSBC	banks – retail	73.0	4.0
5	Glaxo Wellcome	pharmaceutical	63.7	3.5
6	Shell	oil	51.2	2.8
7	Astrazeneca	pharmaceutical	45.6	2.5
8	SmithKline Beecham	pharmaceutical	44.4	2.4
9	Lloyds TSB Group	banks – retail	42.4	2.3
10	Marconi	electronics	29.8	1.6
Total			665.2	36.5

Source: Financial Times, 'Markets 2000', 3 January 2000.

times in 1999, which is similar to US experience. This, however, masks the fact that institutions, by far the dominant investors, claim to maintain core shareholdings in the top 200 or so companies for just over eight years on average according to research sponsored by the Investors Relations Society.[7] If so, other shareholders are turning over their portfolios much more rapidly than just over two years, implying a high rate of change. Given that the dealing cost averages 0.75 per cent for a purchase (including 0.5 per cent transfer stamp duty) and 0.25 per cent for a sale, i.e. 1 per cent for a typical share swap, this rate of turnover is rather costly, namely £9bn a year (see also Chapter 4).

The total stock market at the end of 1997 was owned approximately as set out in Table 1.3, and is not thought to have altered significantly since then, with the tendency for overseas investment institutions to increase.

There are now an estimated 16.5 million UK citizens who are shareholders, up from 3 million twenty years ago, due to the massive privatizations of the 1980s and early 1990s and the 1990s demutualization of building societies, rather than organic growth. Individuals own over 10 per cent of the top 100 companies and more than 20 per cent of smaller companies

Table 1.3 Ownership of equities, end 1997

	%
Pension funds	26
Life assurance companies	24
Unit and investment trusts	10
Total UK investment institutions	60
Individuals (mainly UK)	20
Overseas (mainly institutions but some foreign governments)	20
	100

Source: 'PDFM pension fund indicators – a long-term perspective on pension fund investment – 1998' and the Final Report of the Hampel Committee on Corporate Governance, January 1998.

This brief analysis shows that shareholder power rests preponderantly with investment institutions, and in particular with domestic pension funds and life assurance companies. If there is to be any active discharge of the ownership role the only candidates are the investment institutions.

The investment institutions are potentially dominant in aggregate, but their individual size is very much smaller than the large companies in which they are invested. The largest pension funds in 1999 are shown in Table 1.4

Insurance companies, and in particular the life insurance companies, are virtually as important as pension funds in their ownership of UK equities at around £310bn at the end of 1998. Published statistics give little breakdown by company. It seems, however, that over half the funds held are attributable to less than fifteen companies, with the Prudential by far the largest. Thus, the number of significant entities are even fewer than for pension funds, but concentrated in larger aggregations.

The beneficial owners of these invested pension and insurance funds, however, comprise over half the population of the UK and the funds are the greater part of their individual savings. Their importance to their owners, and to national wealth and prosperity, cannot be exaggerated.

Table 1.4 Largest UK pension funds, 1999

		£s bn
Public sector		
1	British Coal Corporation	22.9
2	Post Office	17.0
3	BBC	6.3
4	Strathclyde	5.7
5	Greater Manchester	5.6
6	West Midlands Metropolitan Authorities	4.5
		62.0
Private sector		
1	British Telecommunications	24.9
2	Electricity Supply Pension Scheme	19.9
3	Universities	18.8
4	Railways Pensions Trustee Company	14.0
5	BG	12.4
6	Lloyds TSB	12.1
7	BP	10.7
8	Barclays Bank	10.0
9	British Airways	9.6
10	Shell Pensions Trust Ltd	9.4
		141.8

Source: National Association of Pension Funds Year Book, 2000.

The fund managers

In addition to pension funds and insurance companies, there is an important and overlapping third player among the investment institutions: the fund managers. These are the specialist financial firms who invest funds on behalf of institutions which are intermediaries between savers and users of capital.[8] They are a conspicuously successful part of Britain's financial sector. The great bulk of the funds they invest comes from pension funds (nearly 50 per cent) and insurance companies (25 per cent), the dominant investment institutions. Unit and investment trusts account for a further 11 per cent, and the remaining 15 per cent from a variety of sources, including individuals (nearly 5 per cent). Less than 10 per cent of pension funds are managed internally, the rest are in the hands of external fund managers. Over three-quarters of fund managers are owned broadly equally by investment banks and insurance companies, 58 per cent being British and 42 per cent foreign owned. However, independently owned managers are increasingly being acquired, primarily by investment banks, particularly American and, to a lesser extent, European. It is big business worldwide and has high prospects of long-term gains as populations age, grow wealthier and save for retirement, and as governments in most Western countries seek to switch unfunded state pensions more into funded 'stakeholder' pensions. Furthermore, fund management has more stable earnings than most investment banking activities. For all these reasons fund management is a particularly attractive financial business sector in which to participate.

Insurance companies, apart from the smaller ones, usually invest not only their own very large funds (principally of policyholders), but also pension funds of companies and various public sector bodies. They are thus both direct institutional investors and fund managers.

The main task of fund managers is to allocate the huge volume of assets in their care, plus the cash flows generated from savers, policyholders' insurance premiums and pension contributions. While terms of investment are always agreed with clients, it is the fund managers who have the prime responsibility for choosing from the wide range of financial investments (which is their special expertise) that balance of risk and reward best suited to client needs. They unquestionably exercise great power in determining investment decisions. Their top managers and specialists are amongst the highest paid people in Britain, and certainly equal to most of the highly paid senior managers elsewhere.

Funds under management totalled £2,170bn in July 1999, £1,598bn for domestic clients and £572bn for overseas clients.[9] Equities comprise 63 per cent of funds managed, bonds 25 per cent, with property, cash and 'other' making up the remaining 12 per cent.

The industry is very concentrated. Of the seventy-nine members of the Institute of Fund Managers supplying annual statistics, the top quartile now manage 65 per cent of the business (69 per cent in 1998). This concentration may change again as fund management becomes a truly global industry, with US firms being by far the strongest players and major purchasers.

Table 1.5 Largest pension fund managers

	Segregated funds (£s bn)	Total funds managed (£s bn)
Mercury Asset Management	67	115
Schroder Investment Management	61	119
Phillips & Drew Fund Management	46	54
Barclays Global Investors	40	370
Morgan Grenfell Asset Management	25	103
Sub total	239	761
Totals – top 25	385	2539

Source: 'Pension Fund Investment', *Financial Times* Supplement, 21 May 1999.

The five largest segregated pension fund managers at the end of 1998, out of the top twenty-five firms, dominated their industry (Table 1.5).

The top four were thus 56 per cent of the segregated funds, or 62 per cent including the dominant 'passive' manager (Barclays), and the top five were 30 per cent of total funds managed. This is concentration indeed, but experts now believe that it has peaked. This is because in 1998 and 1999 the largest active managers all hit performance troubles, and started to lose contracts to smaller managers and to passive managers.

Passive managers allocate share investment according to predetermined stock market indices. They have lower costs because their portfolios largely avoid transaction costs, and management costs are significantly lower. Active managers have higher costs in both areas (and the superstar salaries and bonuses). They aim to achieve higher values by selective stock picking and asset allocations between different stock and financial instruments often worldwide. During the later stages of prolonged bull markets, passive managers generally have the edge. Over the three years to end-1999 they have outperformed the largest fund managers, in some cases by a considerable margin. In consequence they have been growing relative to active managers and now have about 25 per cent of the total market (35 per cent in America) from a standing start twenty-five years ago. (Barclays Global Investors quoted above are the world's largest index tracker.) The difficulty for pension fund clients is that passive managers are effectively 'blind' and must follow overheated bull markets no matter how extreme they become. Likewise they must follow bear markets down. In both cases they add to market volatility, a generally unwelcome characteristic. A further problem arises because of the relative growth of a handful of mega companies (see above) to become a large part of total market capitalization. Passive funds (also known as 'tracker funds') inevitably forfeit a widely spread portfolio which may temper their relative growth.

The longer the period over which comparisons are made between the two styles of fund, the better the best active managers can be expected to perform. Schroders, whose funds have generally beaten the stock market averages over ten-year periods, argues strongly for a period of comparison over a full economic cycle.[10] With fund managers being increasingly judged over periods of three years or less (Chapters 2 and 4), the opportunity to demonstrate better performance is often denied. Investment institutions and pension fund trustees, advised by their consulting actuaries, pay much attention to specialized published quarterly performance measures. Increasingly fund managers are changed for not beating median or higher performances over only a few years.

Schroders believes the best active managers can outperform by superior stock selection, and even more by superior asset allocation. Passive funds cannot avoid crucial choices such as which particular stock market index to track, and, still less, asset allocation between different financial instruments and different markets. The different risk and return profiles of the two approaches often results in particular funds combining them to secure more even investment returns over an economic cycle. Hence the gap between active and passive managers is lessening, as active investors have to hold most of the top 100 companies which exceed three-quarters of the market. They are increasingly becoming 'closet indexers'. Given the growing similarity of most investment portfolios, little and sometimes no benefit may accrue, making short-term judgements on performance even more unsatisfactory.[11] This situation has an important bearing on effective remedies for absentee ownership discussed in Chapter 8.

Boards' composition and accountability

The traditional model of corporate governance is that publicly quoted companies are run primarily in shareholder interests by senior management with closely aligned interests under the control of independent non-executive directors. Many individual spokesmen and investigative committees claim it reflects the underlying reality. A key example of this is the Hampel Committee Report (January 1998) assertion that shareholder interests should predominate in corporate governance since they own the companies and '*appoint the directors*' (1.15, my italics). If this latter point is not mainly true, then all the conclusions based on it are seriously undermined. Since the 1930s, in Britain and America entrepreneurial (often family) capitalism gave way first to mainly individual (and thus powerless) shareholders, with none having a sufficient interest at stake remotely to cover the costs of activism. From the 1960s onwards this gave way in turn to the rise of investment institutions to dominance (Table 1.3) as both occupational pensions and personal pensions became the main channel for individual investment, with the huge advantage of cheap, widely spread (lower-risk) long-term equity investment. While these institutions have the potential to exercise the shareholders' (ownership) power, in practice they have seldom done so, save in the comparatively rare case of serious underperformance or corporate crisis.

The main interest of the institutions is the risk, make-up and performance of their widely spread investment portfolios as a whole. Fund managers in particular cherish the freedom to buy and sell shares at will, since they are in fierce competition with each other to attract and retain funds. The inescapable result is that the ownership role is not actively discharged. We have a system of largely absentee owners. We do not lack long-term *investors* (see above); most institutions hold core shareholdings in the larger companies for eight years or more. But as ownership duties are seldom actively and, still less, continuously discharged, we lack effective long-term *owners,* i.e. shareholders exercising the interest and influence of controlling shareholders who appoint boards of directors and hold them effectively accountable.

It is a legal requirement to have company directors voted into office by shareholders at annual general meetings. This requirement is met by the existing board members (often by the chairman and CEO) proposing candidates who are then, almost without exception, appointed unanimously by the individual shareholders present. It is usual for institutional shareholders to have given their unanimous consent in advance in the form of a proxy. Very occasionally, in a crisis, investment institutions will have insisted on one or more new candidates, although even in a crisis they will seldom have put forward actual names, merely required some strengthening of the board, usually of its most senior officers.

The Cadbury Report of December 1992 urged institutional investors (4.11) to take a positive interest in the composition of boards of directors. One of the major representatives of the investment institutions immediately disclaimed that this meant putting up candidates. He saw no need for any responsibility for or contact with non-executive directors, a view reflected five years later in the Hampel Report. (A 'positive interest' would seem to be a term of art.) Given that institutional investors will take no direct part in choosing directors, and individual shareholders are quite powerless to do so, it is clear that boards, of necessity, must be self-perpetuating. Many, indeed most, may like it that way, but they cannot fairly be criticized for a situation not of their making.

It should also be noted that the majority of non-executive directors are senior executive directors and often chairman and CEOs of other companies. Thus they share a common view with their executive colleagues which inevitably influences their behaviour and allegiances.

The powerlessness of individual shareholders and the indifference of the institutions means directors are appointed by what Robert Monks has called 'coerced ratification'. At present there is no other way. Nor is it likely to change. The three major governance reports of the last decade, particularly the Cadbury Report, have caused companies increasingly to set up nomination committees for recruiting non-executive candidates, a welcome process. Executive search firms are retained, but the same type of candidate is put up, and it is almost unknown for candidates to be accepted against chairmen/CEO wishes. This system is an improvement, but brings insufficient independence to the process. As nomination committess have no shareholder involvement, they lack ultimate legitimacy. Non-executive directors appointed this way, and I include myself, are chosen, appointed and have our term of office and remuneration fixed by our future colleagues. We, in turn, agree their remuneration, adequacy, period of office, etc. In John Kay's pithy phrase, we have 'the monitored appointing the monitors'. It is hardly an independent, arm's length relationship, and it explains why it is unusual for non-executives in major public companies to take a fully independent line, or resign in protest over some policy matter. Usually only a severe crisis is a sufficient catalyst. This leaves three other forms of accountability. First, and fundamentally, there is the constraint of competitive markets – a government responsibility provision accepted by all political parties. Second, there is continuous scrutiny of most of the top 250 companies by the media, analysts, fund managers, investment banks, etc., based mainly on public knowledge and meetings with top managements. It is undoubtedly fairly effective. Third is the latent or actual threat of takeovers (Chapter 3) which allows share-holders the final say. This is why investment institutions strongly support the process, for it is their only way to change an under-performing management *team*, as opposed to using their influence occasionally to change a CEO. Thus, some strong forces of account-ability exist, but none compare with concerted owner action that can and does arise in, say, venture capital financed companies. The quoted company sector cannot fairly be described as a fully effective market system when the ownership component is so weak.

Executive directors' remuneration

Few subjects in corporate governance attract more comment, most of it hostile, than the remuneration of executive directors, and how it is determined. Directors and their associations, such as the Institute of Directors (IoD), contend that high remuneration is the justified and necessary reward for high risk taking and achieving high performance on which general prosperity, jobs, pensions and public benefits all depend. A frequently made point is that there is a strong international market for the best senior managers which shareholders dare not ignore. Above all else, the system is defended as a natural and key part of the highly successful market system of western capitalism. Sup-porters warn of the palpable dangers of 'interfering with the market', with the clear implication that nothing much is wrong.

The statistical evidence for rapidly rising executive director remuneration is irrefutable, beginning in the mid-1980s, and accelerating throughout the 1990s. The contrast with average earnings is striking. Directors of large companies have created the widest pay gap in Europe compared with their employees, and it is growing. Recent research by the Trades Union Congress submitted to the government's consultation on executive pay in November 1999 found that the average salary for executives in the top 100 British companies was eighteen times that of the average employee (up from twelve times in 1994), or twenty-six times when long-term incentives were included. This compares with 8 to 1 in Germany and 7 to 1 in Sweden, but 24 to 1 in the United States.[12] The contrast was much more marked in the top 100 companies where pay awards to top directors in 1997 were forty-eight times those of average employees. It was more striking still in the top twenty-five British companies where the full package of salary and benefits for CEOs is up to ninety-four times that of the average staff. Only in the United States are figures higher.

Remuneration packages have reached their present high levels by growing at many multiples of average pay increases for 10–15 years, and the process looks set to continue. A highly respected recent survey[13] showed that executive pay is rising at over four times that of national earnings despite repeated government calls for constraint.

The levels of executive director remuneration, while very high on nearly all comparisons with rival nations or the past, may nevertheless be fully or at least partly justified if they reflect very high performance, but this is far from the general case. I reviewed a large number of the relevant British and American professional and academic studies and a representative selection of research publications by the remuneration consultants and major accountancy firms. The conclusions of nearly all the papers, as well as the press articles, were remarkably similar, to the effect that there was little observable correlation with performance, but close correlation with size of company. A point of note from one well-researched article[14] was that the composition of directors' remuneration has greatly altered. In 1985 it was mainly cash (salary and annual bonus). By 1997, after widespread criticism, the breakdown had become roughly a third salary (cash), a fifth in cash bonuses (both annual and sometimes longer), and the rest, nearly 50 per cent, in share options. Herein lies the main explanation for the large increases. UK shares had doubled in the five years before the article, and have risen by a further 25 per cent to end 1999. But price–earnings (P/E) ratios have increased from around 10–12 in the mid -1980s to 22 in 1998 to over 30 by end 1999. (P/E ratios in the major international growth stocks such as pharmaceuticals and telecoms are often more than 50, and much higher for some fashionable high technology stocks.) In other words shares generally were very significantly re-rated by the stock market and rose at three times the rate of earnings. Senior executives, with much more of their remuneration in the form of stock options and share price related bonuses, have thus been the major beneficiaries, not primarily for *achieved* earnings but from a market *general re-rating* of stocks over which they had little influence. Their performance, viewed in this light, is thus much less impressive than generally believed. It may be argued that investors should have no concerns because they have seen share prices soar. But stock options (Chapter 2) do not align shareholder and management interests too well. They are risk-free one-way bets. And once cashed, nothing has to be handed back even if share prices later fall or collapse.

One of the best, fairest and most succinct assessments on the relationship between performance and high pay comes from Ruth Lea, Head of the Policy Unit at the IoD.[15] The main research literature and consultants' reports are admirably summarized. As the IoD is the respected voice of British directors, it is worth quoting her conclusions based on the reports in full:

> On the basis of the work quoted . . . there seems to be very little correlation between executive pay and company performance. We feel that this lends support to our view that much more needs to be done by way of devising challenging criteria and, as we pointed out . . . we look to the Hampel Committee for guidance. Williams's finding [see below] that there is a positive correlation between shareholdings and performance supports our view that directors should be encouraged to be major shareholders in their companies in order to increase commitment to the long-term success of the company.

The finding of A. P. Williams (in a particularly discerning and fair book which deserves a wide readership)[16] to which Ruth Lea refers was that there was no discernible relationship between executive directors' earnings and either earnings per share or increased shareholder value (share price change plus dividend). He did, however, find a positive correlation between high levels of share *ownership* and high levels of performance, *and the converse*. This important finding is reflected in my proposals (Chapter 8).

Since Williams's book was published, there have been more sophisticated attempts, spurred on by the 1995 Greenbury Report, to produce better long-term incentives, although the average incentive period is only three years, the Greenbury proposed minimum. The Income Data Services 1999 report cited above found 'little relation' between CEO total remuneration and performance, that over half the companies reporting falling profits actually increased remuneration, annual bonuses were weakly linked to profits, less than 3 per cent of the top 350 companies provided the level of disclosure sought by the government, and a quarter of companies did not disclose performance criteria. This is very disappointing since the Cadbury, Greenbury and Hampel reports all emphasized pay should be linked more closely to performance.

At least one influential investor body has responded to the situation. In August 1998 the Association of British Insurers (ABI) issued its 'Guideline Principles for Share-Based Incentive Schemes'. The principle feature is to attempt meaningful, potentially demanding cost disclosure of executive awards to enable shareholders to be better informed. For the first time companies will have to make a serious attempt to evaluate incentives, a welcome development.

Remuneration committees of non-executive directors are now widespread but have proved a mixed blessing to date. A 1999 study (quoted in the *Financial Times*[17]) by Martin Conyon and Simon Peak of the Warwick Business School, studied 94 of the top 100 quoted companies. They established that neither the number of executive directors, nor separation of the chairman/CEO roles were related to compensation levels. Further, the more non-executives on the remuneration committee, the higher the compensation to top managers – an embarrassing finding. Such committees are invariably advised by remuneration consultants, nearly always the same ones advising directors on general management remuneration. They mainly review remuneration of peer groups. As most senior managements aspire to be among their sector's leaders the levels recommended are always above the median, and often in the top quartile, hence the well-known ratcheting effect on re-muneration levels. The consultants, whose main income comes from their general advisory work for the companies, have a clear conflict of interest. They are under pressure not to disappoint their clients. Non-executive directors, nearly always senior executive directors elsewhere, are generally sympathetic to high pay and generous incentives. As they benefit indirectly from a rising remuneration trend which affects their own remuneration, they too have some conflict of interest. They are unlikely to be as tough, demanding and sceptical as informed owners if such entities existed and were active. The pressures to follow the consensus are inevitably very strong.

The final point to consider is the extent to which executive directors' remuneration can fairly be described as the natural workings of the market. Analogies with sporting or entertainment stars, whose worth is constantly tested in the world's most competitive market, are quite misplaced. The same applies to the earnings of successful entrepreneurs who have created profitable major firms and taken high personal risks. The determination of senior executive remuneration is not a direct market process, but is based on necessarily imperfect comparisons, and involves significant conflicts of interest.

Management performance can be judged only over some years, and it is not easy to determine individual contributions to what is inescapably a team effort. Key research in the area[18] has shown that the undoubted market for top managers is, by its very nature, an imperfect one. Neither executive nor non-executive directors can be blamed for this situation. It results from the lack of involvement of owners who alone can confer real objectivity, independence and, not least, full legitimacy.

The same paper confirms other research showing that the inter-national market for executives is a narrow one, and that international mobility among top executives is very small. Most of it has been a one-way traffic from Britain to America, confined to the largest and most internationally orientated companies. Recently, however, a num-ber of underperforming British companies have recruited American CEOs, and had to pay American level rewards.

In sum, the determination of senior executive pay in Britain is less than satisfactory, particularly as it is not strongly linked to performance. It has attracted strong public and employee unease and criticism. If many or even most of the high remuneration *packages* are justified, then only an independent process can confer legitimacy and silence criticism. The present system does not seem either tenable or desirable.

Leaving it all to shareholders, the preferred policy of both the present and past governments, cannot work unless and until corporate governance becomes much more effective.

II

The Weaknesses

CHAPTER 2

Ownership and Management Weaknesses

In the light of the governance overview of contemporary British capitalism in the previous chapter, the resulting main weaknesses are considered over the next four chapters. This chapter concentrates on the most important weaknesses, those relating to ownership and management.

The Cadbury, Greenbury, Myners and Hampel Reports (Chapter 7) have addressed these issues. The government is now actively involved. There has been the recent welcome initiative of the Association of British Insurers (AIB) on linking directors' pay more rigorously to performance. The National Association of Pension Funds (NAPF) has actively encouraged increased voting of institutional shares. This and the subsequent three chapters reinforce these concerns by showing that the main weaknesses are much more deep seated and interdependent than commonly appreciated. They will yield only to more effective remedies than to those advanced to date.

Absentee ownership

Large and overlapping investment portfolios

The main investment institutions, including overseas ones and foreign governments, own up to 80 per cent of British shares. Mainly via fund managers, they hold large concentrations of shares in the top 200 companies which account for 85 per cent of total market capitalization. Crucially and increasingly, these portfolios *largely overlap*. This is true not only of tracker funds (25 per cent of the total and growing) but also of the active funds. The growing size of the mega companies (ten stocks comprise nearly 37 per cent of the market rising to 45 per cent with pending mergers), and the better results of the tracker funds in the last few years of a raging bull market, have caused most active funds to become 'closet indexers' to preserve their business (Chapter 4).

Reluctance to undertake ownership duties

Widespread and largely overlapping investment portfolios result in few institutions holding much in any one company, and inevitably they focus more on the competitive performance of their portfolios as a whole rather than taking a close interest in particular companies. Furthermore, there is an understandable reluctance to undertake the costs and time involved in effective active ownership for a very small percentage of the benefits and 100 per cent of the costs. The over-whelming proportion of the benefits goes to competing rivals. This is the well-known 'free rider' problem. Small wonder that only in a crisis are investment institutions usually willing temporarily to act collect-ively, even though all would benefit from the active and continuing discharge of ownership responsibilities by some entities.

The institutions, and particularly the active fund managers whose success comes from careful stock selection, want to be completely free to trade the shares they hold. If they possessed 'inside' information, this requirement would be seriously restricted. Hence while they regularly meet corporate managements, and make their private judgements on a company's prospects, a really deep exchange of information, discussion and advice which a committed long-term owner would seek and welcome is deliberately avoided. This applies even when a large stake is built up, as happens occasionally, because the motive is speculative, i.e. investment in a company believed to be undervalued. Inside infor-mation could prevent selling down or out at the time of the fund manager's choosing.

Fund managers, especially the largest, have another reason for general passivity. They are fund managers for many of the large pension funds of quoted companies. As such they want to hold on to their existing mandates and they are always seeking new ones. As being an active owner involves holding managements accountable, involvement in remuneration matters, and sometimes seeking major policy changes and top management changes, there is direct conflict of interest between their fund management role and the ownership role. While *in extremis* fund managers can and do stand up to company managements (a few, such as Prudential and Hermes, have a deserved reputation for exercising ownership rights on a regular basis), it cannot be, and is not a process of continuous accountability. The rewarded fund management role prevails over the unrewarded ownership role.

Insurance companies, which have many contacts and business relationships with large companies as well as pension fund management interests, are in much the same position. Pension fund trustees do not have these business conflicts of interest, but it is generally understood that their companies' senior management would not welcome trustees, either directly or via their fund managers, taking an active stance in the affairs of companies in which the pension fund is invested. Corporate managements have a shared interest in trustee passivity.

Thus, for all these reasons, even though the investment institutions own up to 80 per cent of all shares, and have very considerable *latent* powers, the ownership role is seldom actively undertaken save in a crisis. As individual shareholders are also powerless, managements are not effectively accountable to their shareholders on a continuous basis. Active, committed owners are largely absent.

Over-reliance on non-executive directors

The largely passive investment institutions consider management accountability to be the role of 'independent' non-executive directors rather than themselves. As they take no part in choosing such directors, the task falls by default on the executive directors whose nominations are accepted without question. Corporate boards, of necessity, are self-perpetuating, thus flouting a fundamental requirement of any system of governance accountability. The situation would be mitigated if the institutions had high respect for and trust in non-executive directors, but there is some impressive survey evidence, carried out in 1994 for a major accounting firm, which casts doubt on the matter.[1]

Both institutions (84 per cent) and advisers (63 per cent) were disappointed in the effectiveness of non-executive directors *because of their insufficient calibre*. The non-executive directors themselves found lack of time (twenty days or less per annum), lack of knowledge of the business, and insufficient information and consultation with executive colleagues as particular reasons for their own partly acknowledged ineffectiveness. Nearly three-quarters identified a dominant chairman/ CEO as their biggest inhibiting factor.

The protection of shareholders and the role of corporate guardian were almost unanimously seen as the most important duties. The majority felt that non-executives helped to ensure high governance standards, aided by the Cadbury Report's Code of Conduct. Surprisingly, over half the institutions felt non-executives should maintain close contact with themselves, but unsurprisingly two-thirds of executive directors disagreed. (The institutional view is an interesting one since contacts were and are minimal. Institutions do not press for it, and most non-executives would be reluctant to appear disloyal to their executive colleagues.)

The overall findings are both interesting and contradictory. To describe non-executives as not of sufficient calibre when they mainly comprise senior executive directors in other companies is nonsensical. Any ineffectiveness is due to something else. Partly it is the reasons non-executives put forward: the lack of time, information and sufficient consultation, and also over-dominant chairmen/CEOs. As non-executives are appointed only with chairman/CEO support, it takes a major crisis to cause direct confrontational action. Loyalty to one's benefactors (non-executive appointments are generally prized) will obtain on most occasions. But as the interests of shareholders and senior managers often diverge on a number of important matters (compensation, the sense of some takeovers, etc.) non-executives need to be quite free to take an independent line when required, The institutional concern is really dissatisfaction with non-executive independence. But given that investment institutions take no direct part in their appointment, and that non-executives lack the information, time and incentive that full independence would require, the institutions expect too much of non-executive directors. Only unquestioned independence of appointment and active committed shareholders can remedy the present serious weaknesses.

Finance directors' views of investment institutions

Further relevant information is to be found in a more recent (April 1998) survey carried out by *Financial Times* journalists[2] to find out what top directors (mainly finance directors) think of their investors. The directors of the 100 biggest companies were contacted, and an impressive 74 per cent responded. The survey comprised telephone interviews and so not too much weight can be attached to it, but the findings are informative in a field where good research is not plentiful. The very large fund managers (particularly Prudential, Mercury and Schroders) were praised for their knowledge and understanding. The smaller ones were criticized for demanding meetings of little value. A common criticism was the lack of useful comments on the business, its strategy, etc., and a short-term focus.

There were a number of interesting surprises. Eighty-one per cent of directors said the Cadbury and Greenbury corporate governance codes had no effect on investor relationships and were rarely mentioned. Many felt shareholders were too docile, too tolerant of under-performance, and some wished they would be tougher! Ninety-two per cent said shareholders rarely or never tried to use their power to make changes behind the scenes, a direct contradiction to what is so often claimed. Less than a quarter of investors had had any helpful involvement over executive remuneration, 57 per cent being neutral. On voting there was held to be considerably apathy.

Interestingly the biggest shareholders were considered to be long-term investors, who were not pressing to neglect longer-term projects in the interest of short-term profits. There is, however, a crucial distinction between a passive long-term *investor* and an active, committed long-term *owner*.

Finally, while fund managers sometimes boast of their numerous meetings with companies – and some of the larger ones claim up to a thousand meetings a year – the typical meeting, particularly with companies outside the top 250, is short. The main purpose is to glean information not shared with one's competitors. The focus is on dividends and short-term prospects. These are far from strategic meetings where ownership responsibilities are exercised: the main purpose is to gather information on whether to adjust one's portfolio. In fairness, the meetings of the large fund managers with the top companies are much more informative and strategic, and have improved considerably in the last few years. But they are hardly 'owners' meetings, not least because fund managers attend singly, not in a critical mass.

Disenfranchised beneficial owners

The investment institutions (the pension funds, insurance companies, investment and unit trusts) are the legal owners of their shares, but the *beneficial* owners are the individual members of the pension schemes, the policyholders, the investment trust shareholders and the holders of units. These beneficial owners have little say in how their funds are invested. This is inescapable given their large numbers (15 million plus) and the fact that they are investing collectively. It is clear, however, that the shares held by the investment institutions should be invested to maximize the long-term interests of this group. On the outcome of such investments the greater part of the nation's non-government provision of retirement income depends, a dependency which will grow in importance as state welfare and pension provisions shrink. For the average household, life assurance policies and pension entitlements are their most important asset, worth half as much again as their houses.[3] How well and at what cost they are invested is of crucial personal and national importance. This raises the question of the accountability of the investment institutions to their beneficiaries. Insurance companies have no trustees looking after policyholders' interests. Thus responsibility lies with the directors. The last five years, however, have resulted in widespread unease at the mis-selling of many pensions, onerous annual charges, etc., to the extent that many people are now reluctant to trust them with their major savings (Chapter 5).

Corporate pensions have been better handled. Under the still dominant defined benefit (DB) schemes the worth of such pensions depends primarily on the employer's guarantee rather than the performance of the pension funds for which the pension trustees are responsible. But the pressure on employers to shift the growing investment risks of DB schemes onto employees via defined contribution (DC) schemes is growing and may become irresistible (Chapter 5). Further, employees have a major and legitimate interest in the investment performance of their company's scheme because companies merge or are taken over, and some fail. In such cases the value and performance of the pension fund is the ultimate guarantor of their pension. As such, employees are entitled to regard pension fund trustees as their guardians, and have a clear interest in their performance.

Until recent years pension fund trustees have been management dominated because companies mainly bear the pension risk. But trustees are becoming more independent. At least a third of trustees must be employees or pension fund members and it is quite common for some trustees to be independent. The rest will be management nominees, usually including the financial director. Because of the corporate guarantee, the management nominee has the last say in key matters such as appointing fund managers, but even so *all* trustees are required to act in the best interest of the beneficiaries at all times. The critical governance point (see above), however, is that there is no history or expectation that pension fund trustees will exercise any active ownership role in relation to the shares held. That has never been seen as their role and it would be frowned upon by their corporate managements. Hence the large part of institutional investor funds owned by pension funds are not usually involved in discharging ownership responsibilities.

In sum, pension fund trustees and life assurance companies are still far from being significantly accountable to their beneficiaries.

Unsatisfactory fund management contracts

One of the most significant weaknesses of present corporate governance is the mismatch between the periods over which fund managers are judged and the rather longer periods which might be in beneficiaries' interests. Beneficiaries are very long-term investors essentially saving for retirement. But trustees effectively impose relatively short time horizons. While the contracts of fund managers typically run for five or six years they would become concerned at the prospect of either dismissal or the loss of a large part of their investment fund responsibilities if their performance for a client as measured quarterly were not to be in the top quartile over the previous two or three years.

Inevitably, this causes fund managers to favour shares expected to perform well on a short-term basis, which puts indirect but significant pressure on many corporate managements to pay more attention to short-term share performance. This, coupled with widely dispersed share portfolios, can weaken investor support for otherwise justified longer-term corporate policies. There are thus few incentives for fund managers to take as long term a view as either their investment skills justify if only they could rely on longer-term loyalty from their clients, or as may be in the interests of beneficiaries. This unsatisfactory situation underlies one of the main accusations of short-termism. It is more fully covered in Chapter 4.

There is some cogent evidence that the more frequent changing of fund managers to those showing the best recent short-term performance is often wasteful. An October 1998 study by WM,[4] the performance measurement specialist, showed that 60 per cent of the seventy-seven pension funds who had changed their 'active' managers in the past ten years had experienced worst performance as a result. While most had been changed because they had underperformed other managers, in the three years after the change the newcomers under-performed the previous incumbents! The typical cost of changing managers is estimated at 2 per cent, a large enough sum to affect performance. Further, a new manager's portfolio selection will seldom be too different from its predecessor for the reasons set out earlier.

The time has come for pension fund trustees to reconsider their practices in judging fund managers over too short a period, and changing them too frequently for an often worse result. The same applies to their actuarial advisers who, by their training and instincts, ought to have a more relevant longer-term perspective. Both should consider the benefits from lengthened fund management contracts to an expected period of, say, five years, subject to safeguards. This would be welcomed by fund managements who would be freed to take longer-term views where justified. It would also complement the development of five-year long-term incentive schemes for corporate managements (presently more usually three years) and thus encourage longer-term corporate policies where desirable and justified (Chapters 4 and 8), thus serving better the interests of the ultimate beneficiaries.

Inadequate management accountability

One of the most criticized and inescapable consequences of absentee ownership is the lack of effective management accountability. Where this is not the case management actions will inevitably become self-serving to a greater or lesser degree. There may eventually be a revolt against them. As Burke remarked, 'All governance depends ultimately on the consent of the governed.'

Perceived management remuneration abuse

The legitimacy of present corporate governance is being increasingly and widely questioned because of perceived management remuneration abuse. Directors' rewards are on a steeply rising trend largely divorced from managers, employees, risk taking and corporate performance (particularly profits), sanctioned by remuneration committees of their peers whose legitimacy and independence is increasingly disputed. The typical three-year long-term incentive (LTI) period bears too little relationship to business realities in many industries.

Dissatisfaction has grown with lack of transparency. Greenbury urged the need for complete disclosure of all remuneration benefits, including the cost of executive director pensions, one of the largest components of remuneration. Job changers usually lose out on pension entitlements (Chapter 5). To attract high-fliers, therefore, companies increasingly offer to make up pension rights that have been foregone. Further, as high-fliers usually receive handsome pay rises both initially and subsequently, the cost of providing pensions at two-thirds of final salary – the norm in senior posts – can be very expensive. The nearer to retirement and the higher the pay, the more costs rise. (A typical £50,000 salary rise can require six or seven times this amount to be put into the firm's pension fund, say £300,000–350,000.) Greenbury wanted both sums disclosed in the annual report. Because even by 1995 public criticism of 'fat cats' was high, this recommended disclosure was fiercely opposed by various management organizations, who feared a public outcry when full costs were revealed.

It was eventually resolved, after heated debate, to allow either full cost disclosure or to provide sufficient information from which costs might be deduced. Many firms were confident that costs could be justified to shareholders. Others took refuge in the permitted obscurity. It has been an unedifying process, damaging many senior managements. Free markets depend on full information for effectiveness. So too does corporate government legitimacy. There is no justification for hiding from shareholders how their money is being spent.

It is ironic to note that directors' fears of adverse publicity from full disclosure were quite misplaced. Companies giving full details were not criticized over the amounts. Those who obscured the costs were not criticized for withholding them, despite the often very large sums involved. It is a powerful demonstration of the lack of shareholder power or even interest. And, as discussed earlier, most fund managers and investment institutions have their own reasons for keeping a low profile. Managements can be forgiven for taking silence for shareholders' approval. Until effective means are found to reflect the interests of individual shareholders and beneficiaries (Chapter 8) little will change.

Mega companies beyond effective control

The previous chapter set out the market capitalization of Britain's largest companies at the end of 1999. The top ten comprised nearly 37 per cent of the whole market and nearly 48 per cent of the value of the top 100 companies (which were 77 per cent of total market). The values of the ten ranged between £30bn to over £120bn, and their combined value was £665bn, a figure which planned mega mergers will increase. The value of even the major pension funds is much smaller. The top ten by size ranged between £10bn and £23bn, a total value of £163bn. It is reasonable to assume that perhaps half their total funds were in British equities, making individual holdings in the range £5–12bn, perhaps £80bn in total. Policyholders' funds in a few of the biggest insurance companies considerably exceed the individual pension fund figures, but no precise breakdown is available.

These figures show that even the largest investment institutions could have only a few per cent in the shares of the very largest companies or mega companies. The same applies, to a lesser extent, to the very large fund managers. Thus, as long as shareholdings are widely spread, and co-operative action rare, the largest companies are beyond shareholder control. Power has effectively passed to self-perpetuating boards of directors because absentee ownership has created a vacuum which had to be filled. Given general shareholder apathy, the same applies to most of the rest of the top 100. It explains why the very large companies, the IBMs and the GECs, underperformed for many years without interference. Paying lip service to shareholder value usually sufficed.

A fairly striking example of institutional shareholder powerlessness was the planned pharmaceutical merger in early 1998 between Glaxo Wellcome (Glaxo) and SmithKline Beecham (SKB) – a merger set to be consummated in the first half of 2000. Glaxo was then Britain's highest valued company (£52bn) and SKB (£34bn) was sixth – or £86bn combined. The market expected an additional £20bn of shareholder value. At the last moment the merger was called off because of disagreement over the top management positions. As management harmony is vital in a merger, to break off was not necessarily wrong. The astonishing point from a shareholder perspective, however, is that no institutional or fund management power was exercised to attempt reconsideration despite the huge prospective gain, and the ability handsomely to compensate management losers – yet the institutions were by far the majority shareholders. Virtually every institution and fund manager must have had sizeable holdings in both companies. Even so, their *latent* power was unable to match that of the two corporate managements. It would be hard to find a more telling example of lack of management accountability. Mega companies are clearly their own masters.

As even large governments sometimes seem powerless in the face of mega companies, the lack of management accountability to shareholders or anyone else is a matter of major concern. Corporate governance reform needs to comprehend even such companies as these (Chapter 8).

Consultants too close to managements

Finally, management accountability is quite unsatisfactory as regards the appointment of both auditors and executive remuneration consultants.

The clear legal right of shareholders to elect auditors at each AGM is usually a mere formality. Management nominates the auditors, nearly always to reappoint the incumbent, and routinely this is unanimously approved. But the accountants, especially the dominant big five global firms, have become predominantly consultants. Their consultancy fees usually dwarf the audit fees to their clients, causing a major conflict of interest. It is harder for auditors to deal with managements at arm's length. This is not to impugn auditor integrity, but the situation is quite unsatisfactory.

The best way to resolve the difficulties is to avoid them altogether. Accounting firms should not be consultants where they are also the auditors. This would involve no overall loss of business as accountancy firms would give up some business and pick it up from other companies. Alternatively, they could well prefer to split off their auditing arms into a separate business, as is now beginning to happen.[5] Regardless of how the split off of independent auditors occurs, the audit committee of truly independent non-executive directors alone should nominate auditors to shareholders for one of an auditor's main duties is to report on the stewardship of the management.

The same logic should apply to remuneration consultants. Such consultants also look to managements as their dominant clients, as they usually advise on managerial remuneration and incentives on a company-wide basis. There is a clear conflict of interest if they also advise the remuneration committee on executive directors' remuneration and incentives. The conflict of interest is as obvious as the remedy. Remuneration committees should be independently advised by consultants of their own choice. Again, in aggregate, there would be no loss of business to the consultants, merely a rearrangement of clients.

Overcoming both these weaknesses requires fully independent non-executive directors linked to shareholders (see Chapter 8).

Taking companies private

No review of the weaknesses of British capitalism would be complete without considering the significant and growing trend to take more quoted companies private. The trend is an implied criticism of absentee ownership, and a return to the strengths and virtues of owner-capitalism. It is a reaction to fund managers and institutions being interested increasingly only in the top 200 quoted companies, which comprise 85 per cent of market valuation. The rest are ceasing to have much appeal. Indeed, the market is seemingly also losing interest in many of the 100 companies below the top 100 whose stock market values languish.

Companies are taken or kept private because they are more profitable than if quoted, indeed often very much more profitable. The average annual returns for the past five years published regularly by the British Venture Capital Association are 2–2.5 times those of investment institutions on quoted shares. There are two main forms of generally successful private companies:

- formerly underperforming divisions of the non-core activities of major firms; and
- companies valued at less than £1bn.

The latter companies can often flourish only in more stable conditions or over a longer term than interests most fund managers.

The success of so many buy-out companies prompted *The Times* City Editor to wonder why the 'rejects' can so outperform their parents under different ownership.[6] Why do largely unchanged management teams, who often considered themselves moderate performers, flourish under venture capitalism? My answer from direct experience as well as observation is that risk-taking owner-managers, with generous incentives, clearly linked to longer-term performance, and financial backing, have the preconditions for superior performance.

The same conclusion applies to taking companies private. This happens when the stock market valuation is significantly below that of their managements and venture capital ('private equity') backers. It is much easier to convince one or two committed longer-term private backers if profits have been volatile for a few years, than numerous analysts and fund managers. And every major stock market fall increases the supply of available non-core divisions and subsidiaries of quoted companies available for refinancing by venture capital firms with secure long-term finance. Hence, they will continue to flourish and grow.

It is reassuring, if somewhat ironic, to note the well-established and increasing tendency of investment institutions seeking higher returns to invest strongly in venture capital funds. The clear benefits from committed owners with a longer-term perspective and more effective management incentives point to the significant gains available if these conditions could be reproduced for the main quoted companies.

The double deficit

It is appropriate at this point to summarize the analysis so far, and to draw out the major implications.

The essence of any system of governance is that those to whom major powers are entrusted must be accountable to those whom they serve. British corporate governance is seen to fail this test.

The legal fiction

The legal intent of corporate governance is that shareholders appoint directors, in particular non-executive directors who are sufficiently independent to hold executive directors fully and satisfactorily account-able. They also appoint the auditors to report on directors' stewardship of companies. This traditional view was summarized in Figure 1 (p. 2).

The reality

The reality is very different. With the pervasiveness of largely absentee ownership, managements are essentially self-governing and self-perpetuating. Most governance power has passed to executive directors, particularly chairman and chief executive officers. The latter effectively choose the non-executive directors, largely from their peers in other companies. They also choose the auditors, the consultants for the executive remuneration committees, and the fund managers for the corporate pension schemes which now own over a quarter of all equities. This represents an unprecedented concentration of corporate governance power in the hands of the very few. Inescapably it has led to widely recognized abuses by executive directors, to often huge remuneration packages poorly related to performance, and to takeovers and mergers frequently driven by managements' motives rather than shareholders' interests (Chapter 3). The remuneration of managements is in large part by share options which are one-way bets, allowing them to share in shareholder success at no financial risk. All this is not efficient free-market capitalism. If owners are not fully in charge of their assets, then the market cannot fulfil its prime requirement of allocating resources efficiently in everyone's interests.

Shareholders in aggregate still possess the latent powers to hold corporate managements accountable, but save in rare crisis or scandal these powers are seldom deployed. They have been neutered by the growth of institutional shareholders (and equivalent) to the point at which they own nearly 80 per cent of all shares and who, with the fund managers, are subject to serious conflicts of interest which seriously hinder their effectiveness in holding management accountable. The result is largely absentee ownership with managements exercising powers in default that properly belong to owners.

The real shareholders

While the investment institutions are the major (80 per cent) share-holders in quoted companies, in fact they are the intermediary agents of the many millions of pension fund members, policyholders, unit trust holders, etc. These beneficiaries are the majority of the ultimate real shareholders whose interests must always be properly considered. But as the investment intermediaries have no effective contact with them, there is little accountability. There are thus two major and reinforcing accountability or democratic deficits. Corporate managements are not effectively accountable to the investment institutions, or the investment institutions to the ultimate shareholders.

The systemic fault

All this is not a criticism of corporate managements, who have necessarily assumed powers relinquished by shareholders. Indeed it is not anyone's fault. Rather it is the consequence of the way the governance system has slowly evolved over many decades with the decline of powerful controlling shareholders. In sum, there is a *systemic* fault. Nearly all the main governance weaknesses are the consequences of this fault, and in particular passive ownership and thus largely unaccountable managements. This analysis was summarized in Figure 2 (p. 5). It has resulted in a corporate governance system in which exec-utive directors, and particularly chairmen and CEOs, are implicitly, in Robert Monks's memorable phrase 'trustees for the public good'. Given the major conflicts of interest, this is a quite inappropriate respon-sibility, but it is the inescapable consequence of the systemic fault.

The principles for effective remedies

The analysis of ownership and management weaknesses suggests the principles on which effective remedies should be based.

Aligning the interests of owners and management

Managements want the preconditions for internationally competitive long-term performance. They also want the legitimized rewards which success merits without the present rising tide of public criticism. Managements' requirements can be made fully compatible with those of the underlying beneficial owners who want optimal long-term returns. (This has been clearly demonstrated for venture capital firms where management incentives have been much more successfully harmonized with investors than in quoted companies.) This implies fairer and longer-term remuneration incentives than the present typically three-year schemes. Present incentives are neither determined by sufficiently independent and independently advised remuneration committees, nor do they align risks with investors. Furthermore, any significant form of long-term ownership commitment is lacking. These handicaps cannot be overcome by managements. Owners need to provide or procure fully independent non-executive directors and the means to provide sufficient, active and committed knowledgeable ownership which would align the interests of both parties. Until then managements will strive to maximize their rewards under present pressures and constraints. One of managements' best present strategies is to increase company size, particularly by mergers and takeovers despite the chequered results for shareholders.[7] (See also Chapter 3.)

The alignment of management risks with investors should involve significant investment in corporate stock rather than no-risk stock options. Many such options have routinely been renegotiated to a lower base when share prices fall, and so are still further away from the risks of investors. Nor do they promote long-term commitment since, once cashed (usually just after the three-year minimum), they cease to be an incentive. Furthermore, under present accounting rules (rightly being reviewed) they appear costless. No charge is made against profits, yet when exercised, all other shareholders are diluted. Compared with America, the amounts are presently small, but it breaches the essential principle of transparency. If options are justified, their true cost should be shown in annual accounts.[8]

Progressive moves are increasingly under way. More companies are moving from stock options to more stretching profit targets which require equalling or exceeding comparable companies' performances. While some require high performance and give appropriate high rewards, many more are widely criticized for being too lax. There is a long way to go before most companies have appropriate schemes linked to high and sustained long-term performance. The key is to produce *sustainable* long-term gains in efficiency and value big enough to be shared by all the corporate 'constituencies'.

These points were cogently argued in a recent article by the American founder of the well-regarded value-based planning advisers, Stern Stewart.[9] He argues that the limited goals of Cadbury, Greenbury and Hampel – transparency, objectivity and best practice[10] – are quite insufficient. Instead the main aims should be to balance the conflicting goals of minimizing cost to shareholders, retaining good managers in a downturn and providing strong incentives for performance. He argues cogently against minimum targets (undesirable in a downturn) and caps which switch off effort when greater gains are possible. In the interests of sustained performance, he advocates deferred bonuses and multi-year targets to lengthen managers' decision-making horizons and encourage continuous improvement – all ideas owners would readily embrace and which independent non-executive directors should implement.

Making ownership worthwhile

The fragmentation of institutional shareholdings into relatively small individual stakes in medium and large companies causes the already referred to 'free rider' problem in which remedial action is not individually worthwhile for most institutions most of the time. But given the clear benefits from committed ownership (longer performance time horizons, reliable support, etc.), it needs to be worth while for at least some of the investment institutions to provide or procure such ownership. This requires that those who undertake such responsibilities and costs should get a fully commensurate *market* reward. A market reward for providing independent non-executive director candidates, and for committing to longer-term ownership, with safeguards from which all shareholders, and particularly the beneficial ones, would gain is essential if effective new investment intermediaries are to be created (Chapter 8).

The merits of more concentrated shareholdings

With widely spread investment portfolios and the resultant 'free rider' problem, apart from an occasional, major corporate crisis, institutional shareholders exercise such powers as they have over individual companies only when they have either to approve a rights issue, or the issue of shares to third parties, or in takeover and merger decisions. There is, however, another way by which selected investors have achieved great success, by following an opposite strategy, i.e. having a concentrated portfolio of only, say, 10–20 shares, which many experts anyway consider to be a sufficient spread if well chosen. It enables the investor to know the companies and the managements well, to have a sufficiently large holding for influence, and frequently, because long-term ownership is the intention, a seat on the board.

Warren Buffet, through his company, Berkshire-Hathaway (BH), is the most celebrated and successful exponent of this strategy, and for thirty years BH has very considerably outperformed the stock market and its rivals. BH takes very large positions, up to 20 per cent (occasionally much more) in a dozen companies whose business they understand, and which are considered likely high performers over twenty years or so – e.g. Coca Cola. Buffett says his favourite time for holding a stock is forever, and the second favourite is for a long time. He usually becomes a director of the company concerned and is highly welcomed by managers and shareholders alike. BH's shares usually trade at a premium to the underlying holdings, a rare if not unique distinction.

Further, and crucially, Buffet negotiates favourable terms for his investment and his expert board participation. Typically he negotiates a convertible preference share on favourable conversion terms if the stock appreciates significantly, and, with his involvement, it usually does.

The BH approach illustrates some critical governance points. First, the long-term commitment and portfolio concentration permit deep knowledge of a company and its strategy. This can lead to high returns well in excess of widely spread portfolios. (BH has earned high and rising *annual* returns in most years as well as superior long-term returns, although there was a significant fall in the volatile stock markets of 1999.[11]) Second, shareholders readily agree both board membership, and favourable investment terms to get the clear benefits from an active, knowledgeable, committed long-term owner. BH thus earns a *market* reward in return for the benefits that accrue to all the other shareholders in the companies concerned.

Warren Buffett has shown the way to overcome absentee ownership and unaccountable managements, and how best to achieve sustainable long-term performance. These principles underlie my remedial proposals – the same principles which have underpinned the success of venture capital funds and taking companies private. The present weaknesses are clearly capable of remedy.

CHAPTER 3

Takeover and Merger Concerns

An inescapable process

The efficient use of resources is a main pillar of capitalism. One of the most important ways to achieve such efficiency is to change the ownership of assets when a new owner is willing to pay more for them than the existing owners. In the case of corporate assets, i.e. companies, this takes the form of either an agreed merger, an agreed takeover (often called a merger in the interest of the morale of the acquired company's management and staff) or a hostile takeover.[1] Fund managers are usually keen to accept most takeover offers – the resultant investment premiums enhance their performance rankings, at least in the short term.

Until the 1990s, hostile takeovers were mainly confined to Britain, America and the rest of the English-speaking world. Until 1995 there had been only four hostile takeovers in Germany since the World War II. Now, however, in Western Europe and Japan, hostile takeovers are occurring more and more frequently as the consequences of the neglect of shareholder interests on corporate efficiency are seen to have extracted too high a price in terms of overall business efficiency and economic growth. Indeed, from the autumn of 1999 onwards, and particularly since the £225bn agreed merger of Vodafone and Mannesman in February 2000, Germany and other major continental companies seem on the threshold of massive change. Hostile takeovers, especially foreign ones, once impossible to imagine, look set to become an accepted and legitimate form of raising corporate performance. This tendency is strongly reinforced by the pressures of globalism and the need to be major participants on American and British stock exchanges.

In fully efficient capital markets and with wise guardianship of the public interest (avoidance of monopolies, etc.) no generally valid criticism of mergers and takeovers can be sustained. The understandable criticisms of those disadvantaged by the process would be accepted as the short-term price for the general long-term benefits resulting. Such changes are inevitable when companies decline in efficiency and fail to satisfy customers. It is wrong to blame the agents of change who merely bring the inescapable changes into sharp focus. Further, many takeovers and mergers are fully justified when a company is performing well but, joined to another, could do better still.

There are two particular criticisms, however, which are well founded. The first is where takeovers or mergers are in the interests of managements but not shareholders. As set out earlier, size is a much surer and quicker route to increasing top management remuneration than long-term performance. The second is when a change of management or strategy or both is required and there is no present way of achieving it, but the often costly, disruptive and usually delayed takeover process. If, however, there are both absentee ownership and insufficiently powerful and independent non-executive directors, the only remaining possibility of change open to dissatisfied shareholders is to wait for a hostile bid. Only a much more efficient system of corporate governance could prevent takeovers and mergers that were not in shareholders' interests, and achieve necessary management or strategy changes more quickly and efficiently. Even then, many takeovers and mergers will be needed and fully justified on grounds of long-term efficiency.

Under the impact of globalization many industries will be forced to consolidate into fewer and much larger firms. As Graham Serjeant observed, 'If America can sustain only two entirely home-grown global car companies, because of the economies of manufacturing design and marketing, surely neither Europe nor Japan can manage more.'[2] He adds that Britain should aim to host and control as many such firms as possible if we are to gain economic strength, a view I fully endorse when companies of enduring value can be created.

A cyclical activity

Reliance on takeovers and mergers as a main form of holding managements accountable and causing desirable changes has serious deficiencies. Apart from the expense, disruption and delays, the process is not a consistent continuous form of pressure. Rather it is highly cyclical. At certain times, usually coinciding with rising markets, there is high activity, e.g. the mid-1960s to early 1970s, 1988/89, 1995, and rising sharply every year from 1998 onwards, with an acceleration in the first quarter of 2000. And the size of deals are far in excess of what was once considered big: £10bn was once a large deal, now £100bn is seen frequently, and some are twice as much again. In between, especially when share prices are falling, the number of takeovers, especially hostile ones, declines markedly, e.g. almost none of significance in 1993. The process is thus a deficient form of accountability, being largely absent perhaps half the time. Further most companies, even in the top 100, and even more in the next 250, are not under actual or potential threat in most years. And it should be noted that merger waves are, like most human activities, affected by fad and fashion. Chief executives, encouraged by deal-hungry investment banks, often think as a class, as do investment institutions. Hence big mergers in particular industries provoke copycat deals in other and quite unrelated industries to demonstrate that their managements' strategies are not behind the times.

A low success rate

Takeovers and mergers may be presently in fashion but studies over the last twenty-five years in Britain and America reveal that well over half, and some suggest even higher proportions, are bad for shareholders.[3] On average, shareholders in acquiring firms often gain little or nothing from these deals, and indeed often lose – the so-called 'winner's curse'.

It should not be too surprising that so many takeovers fail to deliver value. Some, namely those that result from merger wave fashion, lead to numerous doubtful deals. Further the average takeover premium is 35–40 per cent, and can vary from 25 to 50 per cent or even more, depending on the economic cycle and competing bids. Therefore, merely to break even, the acquiring management need to run the firm better by the amount of the premium paid, plus the combined expenses of the two sides (frequently 5 per cent plus of their combined value) plus any disruption costs, which will often include major redundancies. Thus, unless there are genuine and sizeable synergies, typically worth well in excess of the price paid for the acquired company, no gain can result. The frequent failure to make profits from takeovers is therefore understandable. It also explains why mergers are often the preferred strategy as premiums, the main cost, are avoided.

A further major explanation for poor-value mergers and takeovers alike are that the hard part of the process comes after the deal is consummated. Such deals are not always wrong, but they are nearly always risky. As *The Economist* set out in two well-researched articles,[4] the task of putting two formerly independent and usually competing organizations together to achieve the theoretical benefits requires great willpower and management competence, usually beyond all but exceptional managements. It is a difficult, uncomfortable, drawn-out and much misunderstood process with none of the glamour and excitement of the original negotiations. It depends on the two firms agreeing on a clear and sensible strategy and a workable management structure before the deal, requirements that are frequently absent.

There are, of course, many successes or the whole process would have died out. An interesting and comprehensive international 1994 study by a Canadian professor of 1800 manufacturing companies who acquired competing firms between 1988 and 1992 has thrown up some interesting results.[5] Mergers based on economies of scale or to achieve additional market power were often disappointing. But those based on the redeployment of resources, where valuable resources such as technology could not be purchased in the marketplace, strongly correlated with success. But this depended on the fair exchange or sharing of such resources, and being seen to value the people and culture being acquired. If a 'them' and 'us' culture is allowed to emerge, the resultant distrust and demoralization may destroy much, even most of the hoped-for benefits, especially in people-orientated businesses, such as financial services. Undervalued staff simply leave and strengthen the competition, the worst possible outcome.

The most difficult mergers to consummate successfully, for obvious reasons, are those between firms of different nationalities, the 'cross-border' mergers. The large accountancy and consulting firm, KPMG published a report on the subject in November 1999.[6] It was based on a sample of 107 companies from the 700 largest value cross-border deals between 1996 and 1998. Fifty-three per cent of the deals reduced shareholder value, and a further 30 per cent made no discernible difference. These conclusions were based on analysing share prices in relation to competitors in the year after the merger. The evidence of a year is not conclusive but to find that only one deal in six enhanced shareholder value after a year is surprising. It is also a clear warning that mergers driven by the needs of global consolidation will be the hardest to accomplish successfully. Many of the very large and recent oil and drug company mergers have been between largely American and British companies where there is a language and much of a culture in common. They have not been straightforward. Those between Anglo-American and West European firms will be harder again.

The international drug industry is much addicted to mergers, both national and cross-border. They are typically very large companies in their own right, comprising a third of the world's largest twenty-five companies, but by 1999 none had more than 5 per cent of the world market. The case for standing above the merger frenzy was set out in a recent article by David Pilling.[7] The Glaxo/SmithKline and Pfizer/Warner-Lambert mergers give the new companies market shares of 7.5 and 6.5 per cent respectively, compared with Merck at only 5 per cent. But Merck is following the seemingly unfashionable policy of organic growth, eschewing the merger cult of cost-cutting and alleged economies of scale. The current mergers of its main rivals could change that, but since 1994 it has followed its present path successfully. Merck believes the only source of sustainable competitive advantage is major new drug discoveries, depending on knowledge and creativity rather than scale, and it views the future with confidence. It has to be said that the recent history of the drug industry supports the Merck views. According to *The Economist*, few of the 1990s drug mergers produced novel drugs from pooled research, and most failed to add shareholder value.[8] Despite the industry trend to consolidation, the article argued that few made much sense. And marketing alliances, research agreements, better stock management, accelerated drug development, etc., are open to companies on their own.

Complementary arguments were made by Tony Jackson.[9] Drawing on research by the American management consultants A. J. Kearney, merged drug companies are shown to have performed badly, creating significantly less value. Performance by companies merging as much as ten years earlier has typically been worse than before the merger. Jackson also argues that the drug industry is particularly prone to fads and fashions. More worryingly from a governance viewpoint, he argues that however good growth has been – and growth has been good since the mid-1990s, double that of world GDP – shareholders (the institutions) want still more. Hence mergers are partly driven by fear of stock market expectations.

This worry was highlighted in a recent *Financial Times* comment.[10] It pointed out the extraordinary capacity of bullish investors to hold two mutually contradictory views simultaneously. Companies are pushed to mount bids and mergers, driving up their own and other's share prices, yet as soon as a deal is finalized, shares in both companies are marked down, and those of failed bidders marked up!

In sum, the current takeover and merger scene justifies some significant doubts over how efficient and beneficial the processes are for a number of major companies and industries. This is not to cast overall doubt on the whole process. The merger waves of the 1920s created durable successes like ICI and Unilever. The 1960s and 1970s were the reverse, creating many conglomerates without synergies which had to be largely unscrambled in the 1980s to the overall cost of the economy. The City institutions, which urged both processes, as they urge the frantic pace of present mergers and takeovers, earned high fees on what was created only to be dismantled. Their overall advice to companies on the wisdom of takeovers and mergers needs to be treated sceptically.

Who gains?

The prevalence of takeovers and mergers is highly cyclical, but since early 1998 and throughout 1999 and beyond activity has reached new highs. At the start of 2000 activity was at a far higher value, with far larger companies than ever before. To understand what drives this powerful process it is necessary to identify the main gainers. The obvious candidates are the corporate advisers, and in particular the investment banks as they are often also the promoters of deals. Stockbrokers, lawyers and accounting firms are also major beneficiaries but not usually catalytic agents. (The exceptions are the corporate finance departments of the global accounting firms who in effect seek an investment banking role, a further reason to split auditors from accounting consultants.) Corporate finance income is usually by far the largest income category for advisers. It frequently amounts to 5 per cent plus of the total value of bidders and defenders. Unsurprisingly they actively promote such deals to clients, and even to companies not yet clients in the hope of generating highly profitable business. The almost exponential growth of such business in the last few years attests to their success in combination with ambitious corporate managers seeking to increase their companies' size and hence their own remuneration – all this despite the frequent destruction of shareholder value. And all banks and other advisers benefit, since every deal promoted requires an equally large defence team, and every unsound deal will eventually lead to more business when unwound.

These activities raise significant corporate governance issues. The objectivity of equity analysts employed by investment banks is being increasingly questioned, especially in the United States, where the Securities and Exchange Commission has recently voiced serious concerns as commented on by Andrew Hill.[11] Hill points to the near demise of the 'sell' note. He quotes research (by First Call/Thompson Financial, a financial sector research company) of nearly 28,000 individual stock recommendations. Some 69 per cent were 'buy' or 'strong buys', 30 per cent were 'hold', and only 1 per cent were 'sell', a most disturbing development. Analysts are being drawn in to help sales teams to bring in deals. And with fewer and bigger firms, it is sometimes difficult to find analysts not involved in bids or defence.

Corporate boards are virtually obliged to employ advisers. For a company not to employ investment banks, especially when defending against a bid, could be deemed negligent. It would run the risk of lawsuits, especially if US shareholders are involved, as they nearly always are for the larger companies. Advisers, contemplating the high fees involved, cannot be relied on to give disinterested advice. Hence, the need for boards of directors, particularly non-executive directors, to have independent investment banking advice on a continuous basis has never been greater.

Blame for inefficient deals, however, cannot attach to agents, but only to corporate managements. While they seek genuine gains for their companies, other significant factors are involved. Successful deals increase corporate size, power and market security, especially if a mega corporation is created. With the present corporate governance system such companies, as set out earlier, move beyond effective shareholder control. Their chance of a hostile takeover is usually much reduced. It is also a management's quickest and most certain route to greatly enhanced remuneration. I do not argue that there is major managerial abuse, that it is the primary driving force, or that increased size and management responsibilities should go unrewarded. It would, however, be credulous to suppose enhanced remuneration and status play no part in merger/takeover decisions given the evidence of damaged shareholder value in half or more of deals.

Another point of note is that if a management is contemplating a foreign deal, then an American one has an extra appeal. It justifies the top team levelling up to the usually very much higher American remuneration packages without necessarily having to move there and face their much more competitive and unsentimental senior management employment climate. In the BP–Amoco merger, to create the then thirteenth largest global company and the second largest oil company, no one suggested that the senior Amoco executives were too highly paid and should be reduced to the much more modest remuneration that previously had sufficed in BP since that could well have caused an exodus of most senior Americans. Further, for top BP salaries not to match their American counterparts could have demoralized BP's top management. Hence, as international mergers grow in importance perhaps American companies will go at somewhat higher premiums because of this factor – that, after all, is what market forces should dictate.

Identifying effective remedies

The takeover and merger process is a necessary concomitant of efficient market capitalism. It is, however, seen to be riddled with conflicts of interest for managements, investment institutions and corporate advisers. While often beneficial and necessary, there are too many poorly thought out and badly executed deals, many of which owe more to current fads and fashions for more and bigger deals than to business realities. Over half destroy shareholder value. Mergers and, more particularly, takeovers are one of the few means of holding under-performing managements accountable, but they are nevertheless a costly, disruptive and long-delayed means of attempting beneficial changes. The remedy for all these weaknesses and inadequacies is effective disinterested corporate governance. Four matters need to be addressed.

First, it is necessary to be able to evaluate managements better, to strengthen them where possible, to remove them more quickly and cleanly when justified. Only active committed and knowledgeable long-term shareholders can procure or provide these needs. They in turn must appoint fully independent non-executive directors. They would have to be highly capable businesspeople and properly paid for their key responsibilities. As they would owe no obligation to management, they could be expected to initiate management changes more quickly and effectively than at present. Takeovers motivated by the need for management change would be far more infrequent. They should be kept in reserve for when truly needed, i.e. when they are the only effective way. To adapt a cricketing metaphor, takeovers are good longstops but poor wicketkeepers.

Second, when a management wants to mount a bid, defend against one or propose a merger, it should need to make its case to the independent directors given the huge sums at stake, the large disruption of management and employee time and jobs, the conflicts of interest for both management and their advisers, and the high failure rate. The independent directors will need independent advice, and thus long-term relationship advisers free of conflicts of interest. Such advisers should never be involved in bids, defences or mergers for the company they are advising, but rather should be used to evaluate objectively the advice of others. They would need and deserve a large annual retainer fee. Such arrangements are always employed when executive directors seek to buy out their whole company. It is recognized that they have a major conflict of interest. Accordingly, the non-executive directors negotiate on behalf of all shareholders and retain independent advisers. Equally the same principle should apply to the bids and merger proposals of managements, and to their proposed takeover defences. The conflicts of interest are just as great in these cases as in management buyouts.

Third, given that managements are usually gainers from takeovers and mergers, and owners in the acquiring companies are so often losers, it is essential to align their interests. The reasons most MBOs/LBOs are successful is partly for this reason. This should involve *inter alia* executive directors investing in shares held for the long term.

Fourth, and finally, it is desirable that boards occasionally examine the reverse of takeovers and mergers, namely the strength of the case for keeping all or most of the existing activities. This has sometimes happened with the threat of takeover to the clear benefit of share-holders. The interest Hanson took in ICI in the early 1990s forced ICI to hive off its large and successful pharmaceutical business (renamed 'Zeneca') from its traditional bulk chemical business. The same happened to BAT in 1995, subsequent to Goldsmith's failed 1989 bid to split the company, which probably influenced the split into two separately quoted companies, the tobacco and financial interests. This beneficial process should occur on a regular basis, without the need for a takeover threat. Only independent non-executives linked to effective owners could ensure that it happened. Managements (and their head-quarter staffs) often have too much investment in the status quo, not least because remuneration is mainly linked to size, not performance.

The incorporation of these four guidelines into the corporate governance system should largely eliminate the present significant and justified concerns over the takeover and merger process. They would also greatly reduce costs to shareholders and raise corporate perfor-mance. Such major gains are well worth the effort of achieving them.

CHAPTER 4

Short-termism?

Increasingly over the last two decades there have been frequent criticisms of undesirable short-termism levelled against the Anglo-American style of capitalism. Such criticisms must be addressed where any alleged short-termism is caused or aggravated by corporate governance weaknesses, the purpose of this chapter. In particular, this chapter considers the issue of appropriate performance standards for corporate managements, institutional investors and fund managers since the ultimate objective of better corporate governance is to improve such standards.

Inconclusive evidence

The criticisms of Anglo-American capitalism have focused particularly on investment institutions and their fund managers who are said to take only short-term views with damaging consequences for companies and the economy. Similar criticisms are made of corporate managements. Such past criticisms, however, must address the fact of recent massive investment in high technology and internet companies, etc., which can be justified only by *long-term* performance. This would appear to demonstrate a long-term investment view carried to irrational extremes. Huge sums are being invested in companies with little or no profits and, not infrequently, no significant revenues either. The prices to which many of these companies have been bid up will require the most exceptional and sustainable performances over a great many years if they are to prove justified.

Those involved in share investment decisions are not only taking very long-term bets on mainly unproven companies but are also partly selling out of mature, less exciting companies despite their fairly stable earnings and prospects. Therefore it is not possible to equate short-term share investment decisions with investment only in companies with the prospect of short-term earnings performance as opposed to share price expectations. Thus booms can see companies with only very long-term prospects favoured, just as recessions can see overcautious investment mainly in 'fundamental' companies with more assured short-term profit prospects.

All this is not to deny that there are short-term pressures on both corporate and fund managements for suboptimal behaviour, but that it is often dangerous to draw oversimple generalized conclusions. For instance, if it were true that there were a significant number of worthwhile long-term investment opportunities in British and American quoted companies which were being consistently neglected, then a combination of German, Japanese and private equity (venture capital) firms would have been very active in taking them up. In fact, Britain and America have long been the main investors in each others' companies, the Germans and the Japanese have invested mainly in a relatively narrow range of industries, and private equity firms have invested mainly with companies much smaller than the FTSE 100 companies. Further, increasingly over the last decade, it has been the supposedly shorter-term culture of American, and to a lesser extent British, capitalism that has heavily concentrated investment on newer industries with better long-term prospects. Hence the two countries have more of the new mega companies.

What has been increasingly apparent in recent years, however, is that many investment institutions are taking a short-term view of the *share value* prospects of different individual sectors rather than their long-term earnings potential. Given the frequent changes of mind, this has caused increased share price volatility, making investment in shares a riskier business. In sum, the various allegations on short-termism present an inconclusive picture. Coming to firm conclusions is difficult for there is a dearth of reliable statistical studies. Hence this chapter concentrates on the pressures, incentives and conflicts of interest upon the main individual entities, the corporate and fund managements. Each entity is necessarily under pressure to perform over some given period over which it will be judged, and if underperforming, risk being changed. This frequently results in a significant mismatch between the period of judgement and the longer-term interests of the beneficial owners, an issue of considerable importance for corporate governance. The remedy is to ensure no significant entity is incentivized or judged over an inappropriately short period to the detriment of the beneficial shareholders. Only then can markets function efficiently.

Increasing share turnover

The starting point for assessing any short-term pressures is to consider the periods over which shares are held. There are a reasonable amount of data on pension funds which will also largely apply to life insurance companies engaged in the same business.

Currently the whole stock market is changing hands in just under two years.[1] (From Table 1.1, dividing average market capitalization by net turnover the figures are 2.16 in 1997, 2.15 in 1998 and 1.85 in 1999.) That is, on average, nearly half of shares change hands each year. In the mid-1960s turnover was only a third of this rate. But now many investors, especially overseas ones (principally American), trade their portfolios much more actively. And in the last few years there have emerged half a million private investors utilizing their personal computers to speculate via discount brokers.

The statistics for the main investment institutions are quite different from a 50 per cent annual turnover. Pension funds have been switching between a quarter and a third of their equities each year, i.e. holding equities for an average of 3–4 years.[2] PDFM estimated that for pension funds between 1990 and 1998, equities were held for 3–7 years on average. Of course, a large proportion of shares are held for much longer, even indefinitely.

Research by the Investor Relations Society shows investment institutions claim to maintain core shareholdings for just over eight years.[3] This is corroborated by an April 1997 study carried out by an Edinburgh investment performance measurement company, World Markets (WM), and commentated on by Barry Riley.[4] The research was based on the share turnover over six quarters of one large and one small pension fund. Both funds held their core shareholdings over the eighteen months, but traded continuously in them for tactical reasons. By extrapolation, the data suggested pension funds would hold their core shareholdings for eighteen years or so. As the eighteen-year holding period was based on only two funds, and for only eighteen months, it is safer to assume that average core shareholdings are for just eight years, based on the much more detailed research of the Investor Relations Society.

With the whole market changing hands in around two years (the 1997–9 average), all other investors must be trading their holdings much more frequently. Assuming the two main institutions consider 80 per cent of their combined holdings of 60 per cent of UK equities to be core shareholdings (48 per cent of all equities) the remaining 20 per cent of their holdings plus third parties (52 per cent of the market) are being turned over every 1.2 years. For only 60 per cent institutional core holdings, the figure would be 1.4 years. Given the 1 per cent plus combined cost of selling one shareholding, and replacing it by another, these rates of turnover are quite costly. A recent article suggests that both the rate of turnover of institutional shares may now be rather higher, and also transaction costs.[5] As Orton points out, the rate of turnover by investment institutions is far removed from the 'buy and hold' philosophy of Warren Buffett and his Berkshire-Hathaway share-holders. There is little evidence that beneficial investors benefit from the current practices.

Pressures on corporate managements

The investment institutions and fund managers may lack ownership powers, i.e. the ability of hold managements directly accountable (Chapter 2), but in aggregate they have decisive market power to which corporate managements must respond. And the period in which they must respond is getting shorter with the much increased turnover in shares. This is reflected in the fact that chief executives now spend typically only five years in a job. Given this, and the frequently compliant determination of senior management pay by non-executive remuneration committees largely made up of their peers, there is considerable scope for senior management remuneration incentives to diverge from the interests of beneficial shareholders.

In many industries five years is a short time to effect major change. Where capital investment programmes or large expenditures on research and development are needed, the major benefits may well be beyond the typical tenure of a chief executive, particularly if such outlays do not commence in the first year in the job. The need to make a major impact in the period of judgement explains much of the attraction of takeovers and mergers to senior managements, despite their often poor value for shareholders (Chapter 3), compared with usually much slower organic growth. And, remuneration correlates much more with company size than performance (Chapters 1 and 2). There is thus an artificial and undesirable corporate management incentive to acquire or merge with other companies.

Short tenure also explains why the typically so-called long-term incentive (LTI) scheme is usually for only three years. A new CEO and senior management team will take a year or more into the job to formulate the policies on which they are to be judged. This will often be too short a period for considered judgement by either non-executives or the market. But given the pressure for results, particularly bearing in mind that the prime form of remuneration incentives is stock options, there is a further artificial inventive to enhance profitability by shedding staff, limiting profitable longer-term investments, selling off less profitable divisions, buying in shares, etc.

Clearly there are a number of undesirable short-term pressures on corporate managements. Only motivated longer-term owners, via fully independent non-executive directors, would have the incentive and means to effect desirable changes.

Pressures on fund managers

Fund managers are also seen as a prime perpetrators of short-termism. A not untypical recent criticism was that of industrialist Sir John Banham, a former director-general of the CBI, who accused fund managers of being incompetent lemmings in their fashionable pursuit of internet and media stocks.[6] All the principal fund managers were accused of pursuing virtually identical policies, all rushing into and out of the same stocks to the serious detriment of their clients and business as a whole, but at no penalty to themselves. The similar behaviour is largely undeniable but Sir John was accusing the wrong people. The fund managers must follow the investment mandates agreed with their clients, the pension fund trustees and other fiduciaries. It is these mandates, and the period over which fund managers are judged, which causes the consensus action.

At present most fund managers are expected to demonstrate superior performance by three years at the most (often over only two years for an American client) or start to face the risk of dismissal (Chapter 2). This pressure grows without regard to the state of the stock market. Fund managers are forced into copycat investments little different to tracker funds. To have a mistaken investment policy in company with most other major fund managers is still safer than a fundamental value investment policy which may be proved right only belatedly, i.e. when the fund management mandate has been lost to a more conformist house. Christopher Fildes described the present predicament succinctly: 'Originality is out. Diversity, which should be the essence of markets, disappears. . . . Managers chase a small handful of stocks up to silly prices and then hope to sell them to each other.'[7] Thus, there is presently fevered speculation in internet, telecommunication and certain high-technology stocks, many of which have yet to make a profit, and significant selling of most other established stocks.

In these conditions there are fewer and fewer major fund managers who dare to take a contrary position (even though most speculative stocks end in spectacular corrections) causing increased market volatility and risk for all investors. There is thus an increasing disincentive for fund managers to study companies thoroughly, to develop knowledgeable relationships with their managements and to be active in corporate governance. (Tracker funds need do very little in these areas.) These trends are damaging for companies and beneficial investors alike.

Three further short-term pressures on fund managers deserve mention. First, short-term performance pay is increasingly common for their senior staff. Second, the growth of global fund management mergers and acquisitions, particularly by American firms, is increasing, accompanied by increased senior staff turnover. The individuals involved, some of whom move frequently, need to be able to demonstrate shorter-term performance to keep their jobs and to merit the attention of recruiters. Third, there are only three investment consultancy firms who advise the majority of pension fund trustees on the choice, performance and replacement of pension fund managers. As there are so few advisory firms, and their main performance standard is the quarterly league tables with the requirement for fund managers to do well over three years or less, or be at risk, there is too little scope for questioning present trends

The short-term pressures on fund managers are thus almost irresistibly strong, but they cannot remedy matters as the faults lie mainly with their clients.

The pitfalls of long-termism

The undesirable short-term pressures on corporate managements are manifest. There can, however, be too much of the opposite condition of long-termism. American managements suffer as much from short-term pressures as Britain, but have nevertheless responded better to the forces of global competition in this decade than Germany, France and Japan, and most of Asia. One has only to consider America's lead in high-technology industries where the necessity is to be flexible as conditions change quickly. The unfettered, unthinking pursuits of long-term goals, particularly in Japan, have resulted in much long-term investment of low profitability and doubtful merit. Unrealistically low costs of capital have lead to considerably lower capital productivity than America, or even Britain. What matters is that corporate managements should be free to consider, *where fully justified*, longer-term investments which are in the interests of the beneficial owners. The latter are investing mainly for retirement over decades so their time horizons are not a constraint. In practice, it would be sensible for corporate managements to have the possibility of say five-year horizons rather than the three years or so of most of their present long-term incentives, the same period over which fund managers desirably should be judged. But long-termism for its own sake is never justified.

Overcoming the weaknesses

It is apparent that there are numerous constraints putting undesirable short-term pressures on corporate and fund managements. These pressures are not in the best interests of beneficiaries, managements, employees, etc. Such pressures, plus the significant conflicts of interest identified earlier, cause the serious systemic governance fault. Neither corporate nor fund managements are to blame for this, nor do they have the powers to remedy it. The short-term pressures arise because under the present corporate governance system it does not pay the investment institutions, or fund managers, to discharge the ownership role, and both have serious conflicts of interests. Managements perforce are left too much to their own priorities. They lack the benefits of some committed longer-term owners who could discuss, agree and then support the longer-term strategies. Therefore, if possible, a way should be found to discharge the ownership role effectively.

Owners should have the power and incentive to align the remuneration incentives of managements with shareholders. Generous incentives should be provided for, say, five years. Managements should be required to make significant financial commitments and generally share the same risks as investors. (This happens in most management buy-outs and venture capital financed companies to the clear benefit of both managements and investors.) And, owners, via fully independent non-executive directors ensuring that corporate managements' risks and longer-term incentives were properly aligned to shareholders, should not be pressurized into poor-value takeovers, mergers, etc.

Equally there need to be changes in the contracts of fund managers which are the inescapable responsibility of their clients, the pension fund trustees and fiduciaries. Their long-term investment skills abilities must be harnessed by means of extending the *expected* fund management contracts to, say, five years or so, subject to safeguards for unacceptable interim performance. With confidence in a longer period of appointment, fund managers would be able to demonstrate their true investment skills. (Performance over only two or three years is largely random and a poor guide to future performance.) Companies generally would benefit from fund managers able to take a five-year view, and thus able to stand against unsound fads and fashions without hazarding their appointments. The longer periods of contracts should also facilitate fund managers to offer a wider choice of investment policies, not just passive or largely closet index strategies. Hopefully there would be a substantial place for portfolios with fewer but far longer holdings, with close relations with the corporate managements concerned, as with Warren Buffett and Berkshire-Hathaway.

A side benefit from these strategies, in addition to the reasonable expectation of higher long-term returns, would be a lower turnover of shares and less volatility resulting from a better informed stock market from increased interaction between corporate managements and long-term *owners* – as opposed to merely long-term investors.

In sum, improved corporate governance, if achievable, could make a significant difference to the present undesirable short-term pressures on corporate and fund managements to the clear benefit of all participants in the corporate process.

CHAPTER 5

Pension Provision Uncertainties

At present the overwhelming proportion of equities are owned collect-ively, mainly on behalf of employees to provide for their retirement. For most it represents the largest part of their wealth. How pension fund and policyholders' assets are held, and by whom, have major corporate governance implications. At present major changes are in prospect for the future provision of pensions. The UK government, in an attempt to reduce the burden on the public purse, is proposing major changes to the provision of state pensions, including the intro-duction of new forms of government-guided pensions for those in lower-income groups likely to involve major equity investment (the 'stakeholder' pension). The life insurance industry, in the wake of serious mis-selling scandals and widespread criticism of excessively costly and poor-value pensions, is having to rethink its approach to preserve a huge market. And the occupational pension funds, especially those in the private sector, are under increasing pressure to shift more of the the burden of costs and most of the risks onto their individual members. The provision of pensions of all kinds is clearly in the greatest state of flux for a generation. The purpose of this chapter is to assess the impact of the several major prospective changes to determine their corporate governance implications, including a possible significant increase in collectively held equities.

Pension adequacy

The starting point for considering pension provision and the changes coming over the pensions scene is to consider what might constitute an adequate individual pension, and the present prospects for achieving widespread adequacy. Present pension provisions range from 15 per cent of average earnings for those retiring solely on a basic state pension to two-thirds of final salary for a tiny minority of long-stayers under a good occupational pension scheme, a huge range both relatively and absolutely. Pensions experts advise that for funded pensions that anyone intending to retire on 50–67 per cent of final salary needs a 10–15 per cent contribution of annual earnings to a pension fund for the whole of their working lives, depending on investment returns and tax rules. Given that most people's expenditure needs fall significantly when retired, a reasonable target for a pension might be 35–50 per cent of final earnings, with 35 per cent being adequate if other accumulated capital provides some income or benefits. To put matters in perspective, consider the capital sum needed to finance a typical retirement. A married man retiring at sixty-five on a £20,000 annual pension would require an accumulated fund of over £330,000 at current annuity rates based on recent figures,[1] and very much more to inflation proof it. (Annuity rates have halved since 1990 as inflation and interest rates have fallen.) To retire at sixty the cost could rise by 40 per cent plus. From these broad costings the magnitude of the task of providing decent funded pensions will be apparent.

At present there are some 11 million people in occupational pension schemes, and a further nearly 6 million with personal retirement policies with life insurance companies. (Contributions are tax free for employees, employers and individual policyholders.) This leaves 5 million, mainly on incomes in the £9,000–18,000 bracket, with typically no pension provision apart from the small basic state pension. Those in occupational schemes, particularly if in long-term employment, are best placed. Many with personal policies are often quite inadequately covered. The rest are badly provided for. Even with forecast growth rates of pension provision it will be decades before this basic picture alters.

Desired individual pension requiresments

Apart from long-stayers in good long-term final salary pension schemes there is widespread dissatisfaction among employees and the self-employed concerning their likely future pensions. Knowing how to choose sensibly given the bewildering choice of types of policies and providers defeats most people, apart from the financially sophisticated and independently advised. There has been widespread abuse and mis-selling of personal pension policies with slow and often inadequate compensation. Most people, on reaching retirement, are surprised at the smallness of their pensions when they can no longer augment them, particularly those retiring early. Those changing jobs every five years or so – the majority of employees – lose out compared with long-term employees. (Only one in twenty retirees has had thirty years with one employer to build up a pension of 50 per cent or so of final salary.) Finally, pension fund provision has locked away most people's main form of savings for 20–40 years until retirement, making it by far the most inflexible form of saving. Many would have been far better off buying a better home and trading it for a cheaper one on retirement.

The desired individual pension requirements in the light of these dissatisfactions are apparent. People saving for retirement want:

- much more easily understood choices;
- simple and stable *very long-term* tax policies;
- the highest standards of integrity among carefully monitored and regulated providers and advisers;
- fairness between leavers and stayers in occupational schemes and thus the vital ability to change jobs without significant pension penalties;
- far more flexibility in accessing pension entitlements both earlier and in retirement when individual circumstances require it; and
- full confidence that trustees and other fiduciaries are working *solely* and *exclusively* in their beneficiaries' long-term interests (see especially Chapter 8).

If these requirements are not largely met, people will not willingly commit to pension schemes, and huge numbers will continue to be poorly provided for. How pension providers respond to these requirements will largely determine their own futures, and thus who will be the main institutional investors responsible for discharging their corporate governance responsibilities for their beneficiaries.

The main forms of pension provision

It has long been the policy of all governments to encourage pension provision for all citizens as a clearly desirable social aim, and to minimize calls on public revenues. Since World War II, this has taken the form of maximizing private sector provision by numerous tax incentives, etc., but even today, 60 per cent of pensions by value are state provided compared with 40 per cent by the private sector. All governments plan to reverse that dramatically.

State pensions

State pensions began in 1908 when living standards were low and life expectancy for working-class people was only a few years beyond retirement at sixty-five. It was thus understandable that such pensions could then safely be funded from government revenues on a 'pay as you go' basis. There was no obvious need to build up a fund. A modest burden fell on each generation to pay the pensions of the previous generation. Now, nearly a century later, UK state pensions at £35bn are the biggest single item in the social security bill of nearly £100bn. They are funded notionally by employees' National Insurance contributions of up to 10 per cent on incomes up to nearly £28,000 with a further 12.2 per cent arising from employer contributions. These contributions are in effect an employment tax, and in practice are treated merely as a part of government revenues. No investment fund is being built up. Thus each generation continues to pay for the previous generation but the burden is rising steeply. The combination of much earlier retirement and much increased life expectancy has raised the retirement period from two or three years to twenty or so. (Worse still, the ratio of workers to pensioners is set to fall significantly.) Successive governments have sought to limit this burden since 1982 by linking state pensions to retail prices rather than, as previously, the growth of incomes. State pensions are thus falling further and further behind rising living standards. At present they are only 15 per cent of average gross earnings, or slightly less than government guaranteed income support (means-tested poverty relief). They are set to be only 7.5 per cent of average earnings thirty years hence. To be dependent on only a basic state pension in retirement is thus to face penury.

The problem was recognized in 1978 when, in view of the low level of the flat-rate state pension it became compulsory for all employees to pay into a second pension. This could be either a 'state earnings related pension' (SERPS) through National Insurance, or a private scheme or an occupational scheme. Only a third of employees stayed in the poorer value SERPS. The new second state pension just being introduced will, however, be more favourable to the lower paid.

The spectre of the low and declining level of state pensions in the United Kingdom, one of the lowest in Western Europe, has caused concern across the political spectrum since the present situation is clearly unsustainable. (There are some 8 million workers without a second pension.) Proposed solutions are both widely varied and radical. At the end of the 1997 Conservative government, Peter Lilley proposed a particularly radical solution whereby all new entrants to the labour force and their employers would have their basic state pensions replaced by individually owned personal pension policies invested in equities, underpinned by a government guarantee. The New Labour government is not prepared to alter the declining value basic state pension. Instead, it is introducing a regulated form of individual equity-based accounts under savers' direct control intended for even the poorest savers, the 'stakeholder' pension, due to be implemented in 2001. Both schemes give members personal ownership of completely flexible pensions not tied to a particular employer. Inescapably, as with all solutions, the present generation of workers must continue, via taxes, to pay the state pension of their predecessors, while also providing for their own pensions.

Occupational pensions

With 11 million employee members and a further 7.5 million receiving pensions, occupational schemes are the great pensions success story. Whether or not such schemes are provided is a decision for employers, but virtually all public sector employers and large and medium sized businesses provide them. They are understandably the most valued benefit of employees next to salary. Employees are usually asked to contribute up to 6 per cent of salaries, with employers usually paying much more, often 10 per cent, sometimes 12 per cent. On average the combined sums are typically around 15 per cent of salaries, the lifetime annual sums needed (see above) for adequate pension provision.

The schemes are funded and take two main forms. Over 80 per cent (9 million) are 'defined benefit' (DB) schemes, whereby the employer typically guarantees a retirement pension of one-sixtieth of final salary for each year of employment. Forty years service would thus earn two-thirds of final salary, but this level is rarely attained. Even thirty years is achieved only by 5 per cent of employees. However, anyone with twenty years service or more receives a substantial pension compared with all other forms of provision. In DB schemes the legal security for future pensions is the employer's guarantee. The underlying pension fund is in reality a contingency guarantee fund available should the employer cease to be able to pay. Employers are required to make good any deficits on the DB fund, and in equity should equally be allowed to retain any surplus. Recent court decisions, however, have put this in doubt and affected the attraction of DB schemes to employers (see below). (In practice, surpluses have been used to give pension fund holidays to employers and to top up pension deficits of highly paid employees and executive directors.)

DB schemes have trustees, a third of whom represent employees and sometimes retired pensioners. All other members are appointed by management. The chairman of the trustees is frequently the finance director with the major and final decisions in appointing fund managers. Trustees are not at all active in corporate governance over their funds' shareholdings, and their managements would strongly discourage it. In corporate governance terms this effectively sterilizes the 25 per cent of equities owned by pension funds (Chapter 2).

A further 2 million employees (less than 20 per cent) are in money purchase or 'defined contribution' (DC) schemes. Here the employer does not guarantee any final level of pension, but, jointly with employees puts money into a collective pension fund; the eventual payout of pensions will be related to the investment performance of the fund. In practice, employer contributions are often not as generous as in

DB schemes, but even a 3 per cent annual contribution makes DC schemes much better value than personal pension policies. (Tax concessions are available on occupational or personal schemes, but not both for the same individual). DC schemes limit employers' liability to an agreed annual percentage of salary. The investment risk is thus borne entirely by employees. Such schemes are becoming increasingly attractive to employers for reasons set out below. They also are usually better value for those who change jobs frequently since money left behind continues to grow with the pension fund. For long-stayers (twenty years plus) DB schemes are usually superior, especially if stock markets fall in the years before retirement when the value of an individual's fund can fall in a DC scheme, and with it the future pension.

There are, of course, hybrid schemes, e.g. DC schemes with a partial guarantee of pension in relation to salary. Another scheme of growing popularity is the 'group personal pension' (GPP) scheme. This is not, strictly speaking, an occupational pension scheme, but rather a cluster of personal pension schemes, the terms of which are negotiated using the employers' greater bargaining strength and greatly reducing the administrative costs of the providers. Employers contribute as in DC schemes but they have the merit for employees of being fully transferable without penalties. They suit smaller firms with, say, 100 or so employees, and are increasingly used by professional firms such as staff working in law firms (profit-sharing partners make their own arrangements).

Personal pensions

The third main form of pension provision (6 million people) is the personal pension. It is used mainly by the self-employed and those where an employer offers no pension. On average the overall returns on personal pensions have been poor compared with occupational pensions, and sometimes appalling.[2] Partly it arises because of the higher charges involved when dealing with individuals, and partly from the fact that many life insurance companies are not as capable investors as the main fund managers. A major cause of persistent low performance is undoubtedly due to the returns on personal pensions not receiving anything like the same scrutiny as unit trusts until recent years when the serious press has taken a major interest. Because of the bewildering numbers of providers and products, accurate comparisons require much time and expertise. This explains much of the ignorance of policyholders. Wanting to provide for retirement, and knowing that major tax concessions are involved, many nevertheless apply for policies with too little understanding of what is on offer, how to assess charges and surrender values, and whether there are superior alternatives for building up capital for retirement. Most people would be far better off investing in equities via PEPs – now ISAs – because although they attract no tax concessions on sums invested, the proceeds are free of income tax and capital gains tax. This attractive tax shelter makes them the obvious choice for the first tranche of anyone's investment in equities up to the personal annual limits of £7,000, i.e. £14,000 for married couples. (They are also likely to be superior to the planned stakeholder pensions as well as offering the ability to access capital when needed.)

The costs of dealing with individuals are inescapably higher than with groups. Even so, the costs charged on personal pensions have been and are often unreasonably high (as much as 25 per cent overall)[3] and surrender terms are often penal even on policies held for ten years or more. In response, the government has limited annual charges on stakeholder pensions to only 1 per cent and many potential providers are prepared to accept these much lower charges as achievable.

The most damaging action by life insurance companies concerning personal pensions arose from the late 1980s when salesmen wrongly convinced members of occupational pension schemes to switch to personal pensions with their much higher costs and inferior performance, plus the loss of the employers' annual contributions which were usually at least twice that of the employee. (The catalyst was the well-intentioned liberalizing measure of the Conservative government in 1986. This allowed employees to opt out of the previously compulsory requirement to join an employer's pension scheme.) For hundreds of thousands of people the result was disastrous. The New Labour government has compelled the life insurance industry to guarantee repayment of at least £12bn with more to come. The episode has greatly damaged the reputation of life insurance companies and public trust in the worth of providing for retirement by means of personal pensions. Only acceptance that it could never happen again, plus strict and continuous government regulation, can restore public trust. The senior industry spokesman, the Chairman of the Association of British Insur-ers, has frankly admitted the mis-selling should never have happened and will not be allowed to happen again.[4]

The last point of note in this brief outline of the three main forms of pension provision is that both DC schemes and personal pension policies require that the capital fund accumulated at retirement must be invested in an annuity, with the option to take approximately 25 per cent of the fund tax free in cash. With annuity rates having halved in a decade, partly offset by reduced inflation, this has nevertheless resulted in retirees having far lower pensions than expected, yet another major blow. The government is seeking remedies and has meanwhile allowed the take-up of an annuity to be deferred up to the age of seventy-five (and may consider longer), but the disadvantage remains. It requires urgent attention if personal pensions are to remain an acceptable way of providing for retirement.

Future problems and trends

Before assessing the corporate governance implications of likely future forms of pension provision, a brief consideration is needed of certain pressing problems which affect some or all of the three main sources of pensions, and some emerging trends.

A stable taxation regime

It is widely accepted that increased savings for retirement should be encouraged given the poor pension outlook for so many people. A key factor is that everyone should have confidence in a wise and stable pension taxation regime. Until 1998 there had been such stability for decades. Payments into pension schemes could be offset against tax, dividends on pension funds were tax free, no capital gains tax was paid, and the eventual resultant pensions were taxed as income. This encouraged the maximum capital growth of pension funds. The government, suddenly and without consultation, withdrew the tax exemption on UK dividends, and pension funds lost some £5bn a year initially, and a growing amount thereafter. Most experts expect that both share prices and dividends will grow more slowly over the next decade or so than in the past twenty years, making pension fund capital accumulation growth mainly dependent on dividends. As one respected commentator put it, 'this easy almost invisible tax raid has undermined the attraction of pension saving fundamentally'.[5] Without major tax incentives it is not attractive to many people to lock up savings for 30–40 years. The government can choose to tax pension funds, but it cannot choose the consequences. It goes against the stated desire to increase pension provision and it undermines future confidence. If the optimal provision of pensions is to occur, there must clearly be a commitment to a sensible very long-term tax regime for pensions agreed between the major political parties, and preferably the time-tested pre-1998 regime.

Compulsory or voluntary provision

Another key issue on which long-term political agreement is also necessary is whether or not the provision of pensions for individuals should be compulsory, voluntary or some mixture. Participation in the basic state pension has always been compulsory as an undisputed matter of national prudence to avoid individuals depending on state welfare in old age. In recent decades, with the decline in value of the basic pension, it has also applied to minimum second pensions. The withdrawal of the compulsion to join an employer's pension scheme in 1986 (see above) has resulted in 50 per cent of new employees failing to join despite the clear advantages to most of them. The government is unsure whether to make participation in the stakeholder scheme compulsory for lower-income savers; if the scheme is voluntary, there are concerns as to whether it will be taken up sufficiently. In a sense compulsion is involved whatever decision is made. Either individuals are compelled to make some extra provision for themselves, or a future generation of taxpayers will be compelled to provide for them. It is probably right in a liberal society to insist on compulsory pension provision only up to say £25,000–30,000 income, to protect future taxpayers, but no compulsion for higher income levels.

There are no easy answers, but again a visionary long-term policy is required with strong cross-party support to complement a stable pensions tax regime. And strong government regulation of pension providers is always going to be needed to maintain public confidence.

Funding state pensions

One of the most critical of all decisions is whether or not to fund some or all of the basic state pension. Latin American countries, led by Chile in 1981, have pioneered the phasing out of state pensions, with employees building up their own personal pension funds invested in a choice of sensibly regulated unit trusts and with a stable tax regime. It has restored the link between effort and reward, between personal responsibilities and rights, and has proved extremely popular and effective. People save what they wish and have a wide choice of retirement dates. They feel real ownership of their pensions. Savings rates have increased markedly, allowing a significant rise in productive investment and thus economic growth. Pension provision is not tied to a job, hence no penalties occur when changing jobs. There are also sensible arrangements for retirement, avoiding the necessity to purchase only an annuity on the date of retirement. It has been a remarkably successful marriage of the public and private sectors with lessons for all countries, and its success explains why it is being increasingly adopted. Citizens have more confidence in a decent future provision than is possible with a 'pay as you go' state system subject to the whims of successive governments (which led Arthur Seldon of the IEA to describe it wittily and fairly as 'pray as you pay').

It is not necessary to adopt the 'Chilean' system outright. Sweden announced on 1 March 2000 that, in response to an unacceptable future burden on taxes of its state pension commitments, it was introducing major reforms. Of the 18.5 per cent of salaries up to £20,000 that employees pay to the state for a 'pay-as-you-go' basic pension, 2.5 per cent would be invested in their choice of five private sector unit trusts, offering different risk/reward ratios. This 2.5 per cent is expected to raise state pensions significantly over the years. Other nations are undertaking or considering similar experiments.

The form and future of company pensions

The last general pension topic of significance is the future of occupational pension schemes, particularly those of companies. A growing number of people are questioning whether or not corporate pensions will or even should survive in the longer-term. More immediately, the debate is whether or not the existing dominance of the DB scheme should and will give way increasingly to the DC approach. For both employers and employees (apart from long-stayers) DC schemes are becoming increasingly attractive.

There is a powerful general trend in both the public and business spheres to full disclosure of information and to the reduction or elimination of the cross-subsidies that are revealed. In the no-longer staid world of accounting standards there is growing global consensus for full disclosure in published accounts of all corporate assets and liabilities. In particular, the Accounting Standards Board (ASB) is proposing a radical disclosure of the full facts of corporate pensions, including the annual market value of assets compared with liabilities. With pension funds mainly invested in equities and with an increasingly volatile stock market, there will be marked fluctuations in asset value. Companies will have to disclose what they will hope are only temporary deficits with consequent effects on the market price and hence volatility of their own share prices. This situation has been greatly aggravated in the United Kingdom by the 1995 Pensions Act, which compels disclosure of a minimum fund matched to the liabilities. All this is causing companies to be much more conscious of the risks and inconveniences of DB pension schemes. Risk awareness is already causing a shift from mainly equities to a significant proportion of bonds. But for many long-term pension funds that is not an attractive option. Accordingly, finance directors and their colleagues are increasingly conscious of the benefits to their companies from switching to DC schemes whereby liability is limited to the annual payment into the pension fund. The investment risk is transferred to employees and stock market fluctuations no longer threaten an unwelcome impact on company accounts. A potentially huge long-term liability is avoided. So too is the need for unpredictable and sizeable cash calls to top up the minimum funding requirement. The pressures on employers to switch to DC schemes are now very powerful.[6]

The article in *The Economist* argued that the case for money purchase schemes rests on more than shareholder value. Increasingly they are seen as the only type of occupational scheme that fits modern employment conditions. The DB approach was suited to earlier decades where staying long-term with one employer was the norm for salaried employees. Now people change jobs and homes far more often and companies restructure, down-size, move location, etc., with increasing frequency. Thus, employees as well as employers are drawn more to transferable (or no penalty) pensions. The large cross-subsidies from leavers to stayers, from women to men, and frequently from employees to senior high-fliers (see Chapter 2) are less and less acceptable. As employment stability reduces, and job changing becomes more and more frequent over the next generation – the consensus of employment experts – the move increasingly towards DC schemes is inevitable.

Major employers are increasingly closing their DB scheme to all new staff and are replacing it with a DC or GPP scheme. Many other major employers are preparing to follow suit. Abroad, companies in many significant countries (Switzerland, Australia, Spain, etc.) are also moving the same way. Most importantly, it is the clear trend in the United States (see note 6 above) where frequent job changing is the norm. From near equality in the early 1970s DC schemes are now dominant there. DB schemes are being run down, and although 40 per cent of employees are in them, DC schemes have nearly 50 per cent. This trend was powerfully reinforced in 1978 by a change in US tax law favouring the schemes. The schemes are designated '401(k)' after the relevant clause. The sponsoring employer negotiates with a selection of mutual trust (unit trust) firms to offer a menu of different risk/reward funds from which employees can choose. Mutual trust firms compete strongly for the huge and growing business, and have to market themselves to both individuals and their employers.

Employees are strongly in favour of the development and well-run 401(k) schemes are seen as by far the most important of all employee benefits. They offer endless flexibility to suit individuals of different temperaments and requirements. Younger members go for riskier long-term equities. Those nearing retirement switch more into less risky and less volatile bonds to put a floor under their fund. Well-run 401(k) schemes thus offer individuals far more flexibility than a 'one size fits all' DB scheme. Above all else, employees feel they are in charge of their own future.

It is easy to see why US as well as Chilean experience has been influential on the UK government's stakeholder pension proposals.

Funded pensions to cost more

The Institute of Actuaries is becoming increasingly concerned that the fall in inflation rates, which has been a significant factor in raising stock market valuations, has now ended. Henceforth much lower equity returns are in prospect with major implications for all forms of funded pensions. An official working party of the Institute has recently produced a report, 'Pensions and Low Inflation', which calls attention to a significant likely increase in the costs of funding pensions.[7] The report summarizes its conclusions as 'lower pensions or higher contributions'. Barry Riley comments that actuaries are by nature very cautious and have cried wolf too often in the past. But the clear message is that a 10 per cent contribution of current earnings will buy a much smaller pension than in the past. Pension adequacy will require significantly increased contributions for *all* forms of funded pension, and hence will probably increase future investment in equities.

Corporate governance implications

The ways that the state, occupational and personal provisions have been provided are all undergoing major changes because they no longer sufficiently meet the changed requirements of the individuals concerned (a worldwide trend). While pensions will still largely be purchased *collectively*, albeit from a wider selection of competing providers, those providers will have to tailor their products far more imaginatively to the real needs of the individuals concerned, and in the case of personal pensions, give far better value.

State pensions, for the lower paid, as evidenced by the UK government's stakeholder pension proposals, will increasingly switch to being in part funded by investments (primarily in equities) rather than from tax revenues. They will have to offer value for money, especially if they become partly compulsory, to ensure wide take-up, or there will be a political backlash. But a clear overall effect if the stakeholder scheme is well designed will be greater savings and increased investment in equities. The number of beneficial shareholders will increase dramatically, and with it the need for better corporate governance – see below.

Life insurance companies, and other firms providing personal pensions, will face far more competition. They will have to come up with much simpler, more flexible and better-value products to remain in business. Success will require more standardised, collectively provided products and the demonstrable ability of the insurance company boards to provide or procure effective corporate governance to ensure best value.

Occupational pensions, under the pressures for greater transparency and disclosure, the requirement for full annual market value disclosure of pension fund assets in conjunction with the 1995 Act minimum funding requirement, and employers' growing aversion to unpredictable long-term liabilities and uncontrollably volatile cash calls to make up deficits, will cause companies to switch increasingly from DB to money purchase (DC) pension schemes. Employees will also increasingly prefer such schemes which will be a much better match to the reality of the job market, *providing employers continue to contribute to pension provisions at present DB levels.* Good employers (see Chapter 6) will do this to be sure of attracting and retaining the best staff, and others will have to follow to remain competitive. The unfairness and inflexibilities of present DB schemes will be less and less acceptable to employers and employees alike.

These major changes, including the increasing transfer of the pension investment risk to individuals by both government and employers, are of major corporate governance significance. Individuals will need and want a greater say in how their assets, particularly their dominant equity holdings, are managed as their retirement income will be increasingly dependent on stock market performance. In the case of DC schemes they will seek to be all or at least a majority of the pension fund trustees, and as they will be taking the investment risks, will want investment strategies which best match their long-term needs. They will not accept absentee ownership, the resultant conflicts of interest and the value destroying short-term pressures of contemporary corporate governance. They will look to business, investment intermediaries, pension fund suppliers and ultimately government to ensure their needs are met in an optimal manner (Chapter 7).

In sum, beneficial and direct members of pension schemes, and policyholders, will make the necessary investments for a decent competence in retirement providing they are able to achieve personal control and ownership of their pension provision. And what they own, they will look after far more carefully than present governance arrangements permit. Significant benefits will accrue to pension providers who recognize and respond to the changing market realities.

III

Remedies

CHAPTER 6

Justifying Shareholder Primacy and Superior Governance

In the light of the governance overview of British capitalism in Part I and the analysis of the significant and reinforcing governance weaknesses in Part II, Part III addresses the remedies, both those put forward by others (Chapter 7), and my own proposals (Chapter 8).

The purpose of this chapter is to discuss two important and related matters. The first is to consider whether the traditional guiding principle for running a company, i.e. the maximization of long-term return on capital for shareholders, is a sufficient principle for contemporary capitalism. My conclusion, based on an examination of the evidence, is that it should remain the guiding principle but be applied in the wider context of taking account of the long-term needs of all the other participants whose contribution is vital to long-term corporate success. Companies with this approach do better for their shareholders as well as the other participants. In the light of this conclusion, the second matter is to consider the evidence that superior corporate governance can add significantly to corporate success to the general benefit of all involved.

Shareholders and their values

The starting point of the analysis is to consider precisely who are the shareholders whose interests are either to be maximized or taken into account, and then to identify their values.

The real shareholders

The shareholders to whom directors owe a duty comprise the 20 per cent individual shareholders and the 80 per cent or so of owners whose shares are owned collectively. The ultimate owners of this latter group are the beneficial owners, the millions of pension fund members, insurance company policyholders, members of unit trusts, and the shareholders in investment trusts who together comprise most of the 80 per cent. This group plus the individual shareholders comprise the *real* shareholders whose interests are to be maximized.

It is not the interests of the investment institutions – for they are merely the intermediaries whose clear responsibility is to look after their beneficiaries' interests, and no others. Equally it is not the interests of the many short-term even momentary shareholders (the 'arbitrageurs') mentioned in Bob Monks's Foreword. The maximization of their interests is neither expected nor practicable. If shareholder primacy is justified, therefore, the shareholders concerned can only be the individuals and ultimate beneficiaries, the real shareholders. When directors take decisions in shareholders' name, these are the relevant shareholders. This point is seldom considered when discussing corporate governance. The investment institutions are automatically assumed to be the great majority of shareholders in their own right. The distinction crucially affects the correct identification of shareholders' values.

Shareholders' values and 'shareholder value'

The first point to note about the values of the real shareholders is that they are long-term investors. In the case of the beneficial shareholders, the majority of them are investing over periods of at least ten years, and frequently more than twenty. Given the ups and downs of the stock market, most of the 20 per cent of individual shareholders can also be presumed to have investment horizons of at least five years, the minimum period financial advisers consider sensible for equity investment. Thus it is in the interests of the real shareholders that neither companies nor fund managers should be *artificially* constrained to perform over periods of less than five years. Certainly the typical three-year periods for managers' so-called 'long-term incentives' fail to reflect shareholders' horizons, as does the two- to three-year period over which fund managers are expected to perform if they are not to be under threat (Chapter 4). These represent significant mismatches with the interests of the real shareholders which are likely to affect adversely longer-term corporate performance.

The second significant point is that on occasions there is more to real shareholders' values than 'shareholder value'. It is widely urged that a company's main, even sole, purpose is to maximize the return to shareholders as long as it keeps within the law. No wider obligations are said to be owed to employees, customers, the environment, etc., an attitude which has undoubtedly been the main driving force for seeking a stakeholder approach. Even when a wider duty is acknowledged, the justification is still said to be profit maximization. For example, when neglect of safety by, say, a railway company has resulted in serious casualties, criticisms of the action from shareholder value advocates has been that management's neglect has caused a massive fall in the company's share price from expected major lawsuits and government-imposed penalties to the serious detriment of shareholder value. Such arguments play into the hands of business critics by fulfilling the unfair caricatures of business amorality – and certainly few businessmen would be happy to defend such an argument. The prime reason for giving safety the highest priority in running railways, etc., is that it is right. It is the duty all companies owe to society. The fact that it will usually also be in the long-term interests of shareholders is secondary. Shareholder value cannot take priority over a company's moral duty of care to those affected by its actions, a duty that will often exceed existing laws of regulations. What happens when these aims clash? If, as often alleged, tobacco companies have known and suppressed for decades that smoking is addictive, and thereby have greatly enhanced shareholder value, probably by more than any eventual likely compensation to victims, who would feel that their actions were justified? How comfortable would their shareholders be with such actions taken in their name, particularly when the beneficial shareholders are largely synonymous with the general public and include many smokers? Shareholder value maximization can be justified only when companies behave ethically. This must always include corporate managements being open with their shareholders and stakeholders alike when there is the possibility of serious harm from corporate action. Only when qualified by such duties as these is shareholder value maximization a sufficient guide for corporate conduct.

These points are not a matter of dispute for the overwhelming majority of businessmen. Business, however, is increasingly discredited by arguing that shareholder value maximization is a sufficient guide for all business decisions. Given the serious public decline in business popularity already referred to (Chapter 1), it is in no one's interest to allow the shareholder value criteria to be overstated where it clearly is both an insufficient guide and unfairly damages public respect for business.

Shareholder vs. stakeholder primacy

Consideration can now be given to one of the main issues of contemporary corporate governance, one given new impetus by the election of a New Labour government in 1997 with its support for the 'stakeholder' society.

The candidates

The determination of in whose interests companies should be run is one of the key issues in contemporary British corporate governance. The two main candidates are the long-established maximization of shareholder value, and the stakeholder approach.[1] The latter is defined by its most reasonable advocates as running a company in the interests of its customers, employees, suppliers, local communities, etc., *as well as* its shareholders. In fact, there is a third choice, which the DTI has termed the 'enlightened shareholder' approach. A company can be run in its shareholders' interests while simultaneously recognizing that those interests can be maximized only by taking account of the long-term interests of all the wider groups on whom corporate success depends. This represents my own position and one which I believe can be demonstrated as being in the best long-term interests of all concerned.

Evaluating the choices

The sensible starting point for evaluating the choices is to observe that shareholders receive only the residual earnings of companies after meeting the requirements of customers, suppliers, banks, employees, etc. Maximizing the residual equity reward inescapably requires the enthusiastic long-term co-operation of all these other parties who are paid first. A definition which omits most of the vital contributors is clearly unsatisfactory. The long-term success of any company is clearly the joint product of its management and all these other groups. They must combine fruitfully to make success a reality. It follows that such stakeholders will perform best when welcomed as essential partners rather than treated merely as third parties in a contractual arm's length relationship. This particularly applies to employees and even many managers, groups who often feel they are viewed more as costs to be cut than assets to be maximized. Hence, and the evidence bears this out (see below), co-operation between managements and the wider groups benefits all concerned, not least shareholders.

It must also be strongly emphasized, however, that if the maximization of long-term corporate or shareholder value involves maximizing much more than shareholder interests *it does not involve anything less.* Graham Serjeant put the point well: 'For you will search in vain for companies whose shareholders languish, yet whose other stakeholders prosper.'[2] Financial markets would certainly and rightly desert firms which did not support the principle of maximizing long-term shareholder interests. It is therefore necessary to emphasize an important caveat concerning the conflict of short-term interests between shareholders and stakeholders in aggregate.

The inescapable caveat

It would be totally misleading to suggest that just because companies and their managements need to co-operate with the wider groups to ensure long-term corporate success there are no hard choices to be made between them. To survive and prosper companies must be prepared to adjust all inputs – staff reduction, changing suppliers, ceasing to supply some customers, relocating production, etc. – when economically necessary.

Capitalism thus has two faces. The attractive one is the generation of wealth. The ugly one is market forces, cutting costs, putting other firms out of business, etc.[3] Both faces of capitalism are necessary for progress. This approach, which looks harsh and uncaring, is the only sure way of raising long-term living standards. It frees unproductive workers to move to where their contribution is economic. Without such a discipline, changes in workforce skills and productivity would occur too infrequently and too late, as the poor record of a protected British economy up to the late 1970s bears witness.

The need to take such hard decisions makes it inadvisable to have stakeholder board representation as some have advocated. If stakeholder constituents appointed directors, then decision making would often be difficult and sometimes impossible. Stalemate would inevitably lead to decline and would not serve even the medium-term interests of those concerned. Hence the stakeholder representation model is both impractical and fundamentally flawed. It has no place in effective governance.[4] The shareholder primacy approach is thus the only practicable one. The evidence that it is also in the general long-term interest of stakeholders and shareholders alike is considered next.

The mutual benefits from shareholder primacy

A large number of studies undertaken in Britain and America have concluded that shareholder primacy is in the general long-term interests of all the other stakeholders and particularly employees. Some leading studies are considered in turn.

McKinsey

One of the most thorough and carefully documented studies was by McKinsey.[5] It was undertaken to justify the maximization of shareholder value as a *universal* paramount management goal, and to convince the more sceptical continental European corporate managements. The comprehensive research showed conclusively that a focus on shareholder value is second only to open and competitive product markets in accounting for high productivity, confirming the results of an earlier

McKinsey study[6] of 2,700 companies in twenty countries over ten years. It showed a strong link between shareholder value creation, labour productivity and employment, particularly for Germany, Japan and the United States. The companies creating more shareholder value were both more productive and created more employment growth. In sum, contrary to the majority European view, concentration on shareholder value led to widespread long-term benefits and these were not at the expense of overall employment, a view strongly confirmed in the three and six years since the respective studies. The freer the markets, the more the outcomes moved together for shareholders and employees. In sum, there is strong evidence of a virtuous (reinforcing) cycle linking shareholder and national economic performance.

The McKinsey studies reflected aggregate national corporate governance systems. If America and Britain did better relatively despite the remediable governance weaknesses set out earlier, then improved governance should yield further improvements.

The Centre for Tomorrow's Company

A most useful comprehensive compilation of evidence from a large number of individual Anglo-American corporate studies was published in 1997[7] by the Centre for Tomorrow's Company, an institute well supported by major British companies. Its balanced, fair and objective report makes a convincing case for greater corporate success from the inclusive approach for all participants because it best meets their separate aspirations. It particularly stresses the benefits from valuing employees, the key group in contact with customers and suppliers. Graham Serjeant's just quoted dictum can sensibly also be reversed – whoever heard of a business successful in the long term with disaffected staff? The report quotes a recent MORI study in which 72 per cent of British business leaders agreed that the wider focusing on the interests of the inclusive participants was the best way to further shareholder interests, a significant shift from five years earlier when the Institute began its studies. Another very strong finding was that these leaders believed that only the inclusive approach to worldwide relationships made global success possible and sustainable. Other MORI research has demonstrated, especially for customers and employees, that the most successful relationships moved beyond commitment to spontaneous voluntary advocacy of a company's products, a prize indeed.

A complementary study was made by Professor Richard Hill of the Durham Business School, on the characteristics of companies that began trading before 1800. Of the fifty-seven replies (one-quarter), the common factor was not so much direct concentration on profit (good profits were clearly achieved to permit survival over 200 years) but a core ideology inspiring staff and management, internally promoted CEOs who facilitated rather than directed staff, and an adaptive learning-orientated culture – strong support for the inclusive approach.

The Shell experience

One of Shell's most senior planners reached similar conclusions.[8] Rather unfashionably but persuasively he argued that a company's first duty is survival, and divided companies into the 'living' and the 'economic'. In the former, staff have a strong sense of identity. They are good at learning and adapting, and so survive longer and make more money in the long term (Shell dates from 1890). In contrast, economic companies exist to create wealth primarily for investors and an inner circle of senior managers. They tend to be highly profitable for a limited, often quite short period, and to die young. With such limited purposes (the majority of companies regardless of size) they fare less well in developing either successor managers, or a long lasting community of workers.

De Geus does not argue for the superior virtues of living companies, merely stating that they deliver long-term value to wide communities because they receive sympathy and encouragement, and survive by staying relevant. Most employees and customers prefer such companies which by meeting their long-term needs ensure their loyalties.

Best practice in American industry

The Tomorrow's Company report quotes an interesting Stanford University study of fifty American companies which have been consistently successful over fifty years or more and remain undisputed industry leaders (Merck, Hewlett Packard, Proctor & Gamble, Motorola, 3M, Boeing, etc). Their key distinguishing characteristics included:

- belonging to an elite group;
- historical continuity of value;
- action consistent with stated values and indoctrination of recruits, in such values;
- willingness to take big risks;
- investment in people;
- use of highly challenging goals;
- autonomous operational units;
- objectives beyond profit;
- investment for the long term; and, interestingly,
- no 'saviour' CEO from outside.

Any company in the world would be highly honoured to be included in such a list. It strongly confirms the worth of the long-term commitment to values, people and investment which are the leading characteristics of inclusive companies. The successful approach to long-term shareholder value seems to be clearly enhanced by the wider and co-operative approach rather than the narrow one.

Best practice in British industry

The Tomorrow's Company Report is equally encouraging on best British practice as researched by ISR in 1994.[9]

Staff in 'high morale'/'high performance' companies (the two are found together) attribute their companies' success to management quality, effective communications, and commitment to the best working and safety conditions – although pay and benefits were similar to other companies. The five corporate characteristics which stood out were:

- high regard by customers;
- socially responsible commitment to communities;
- high management interest in staff well-being;
- treating staff with respect and fairness; and
- employees being sure of a job as long as they performed well.

All these attitudes have proved compatible with long-term shareholder value, and indeed have contributed to it. Fund managers and analysts need to be able to identify such characteristics confidently as well as the more obvious financial yardsticks given their correlation to long-term performance.

Shareholders vs. stakeholders – a false dilemma

It should be clear from the quoted British and American evidence that the long-term fortunes of shareholders and stakeholders are not opposed but inextricably linked, a point that deserves to be universally appreciated.

There is a final compelling reason to accept the primacy of long-term shareholder value maximization. The adoption of any other criteria would particularly damage the general long-term interests of all employees. It would cause the value of corporate shares to fall, to the detriment of all investors. Given that over three-quarters of all beneficial shareholders (pension scheme members, policyholders and most individual shareholders) are in fact relying on their investments for retirement, the damage to retirement incomes would be serious. By the time retirement is reached it would be impossible for individuals to rectify the damage. Shareholders, or rather *beneficial* shareholders, are ultimately mainly the same people as employees. It is their vital long-term retirement interests that are being protected by the principle of shareholder primacy, even at a cost of short-term inconvenience for affected workers. Clearly the principle strikes the correct balance.

In sum, companies which reflect the values of the ultimate individual shareholders and which take sympathetic account of the long-term needs of all stakeholders are best placed to maximize long-term shareholder value and to promote a decent society. But even such companies are not immune from either setbacks, periods of major difficulty or even failure. In the last few years Shell, Marks & Spencer and Unipart have all experienced difficulties. Given their values and general approach to customers, employees, local communities, the environment, etc., they all have a better chance of winning through than firms without them. Such values are a good insurance against failures, but not a guarantee.

Cultivating the loyalty dividend

The implicit message of the evidence set out above is that all associated with companies, be they managers, employees, customers, etc., want to be associated with high standards and socially responsible conduct. They want to be valued and provide value. Good leaders throughout history have responded to such needs and been rewarded with loyalty, a factor often neglected in modern business.

Some evidence

A few years ago a refreshing and convincing analysis put the case for the time-honoured approach.[10] Reichheld started by reviewing the common practice of large-scale redundancies to raise profits and productivity quickly. He found them necessary in a third of cases studied, but pointed to the growing evidence that companies *routinely* making large-scale job cuts significantly underperform the market.

Reichheld considered companies adopting the other approach. Two cases illustrate his findings. First, he considered a very successful fast food chain 'Chick-fil-A' with annual growth of 10–15 per cent over the previous decade. Managers get a large fixed share of their branch's profits and are encouraged to seek outside catering business. Most managers stay put and prosper (annual turnover of around 5 per cent compared with a 30–40 per cent industry average) a huge gain for managers, shareholders and the company – the result of a non-traditional career path which creates great staff loyalty by responding to their needs.

The second example concerns customer loyalty. Reichheld cited the policy of the State Farm Insurance Company in the aftermath of a serious 1992 hurricane. The resulting large claims caused many rival companies to refuse renewal insurance to customers. State Farm, in contrast, feeling loyalty should work both ways, paid out more than required to ensure customers could afford new safe roofs – a very sound investment in securing long-term customer loyalty, the prime generator of profits in the insurance industry. Indeed, as Reichheld pointed out, long-term customers buy more, pay more and have fewer bad debts. A 5 per cent rise in customer retention rates can increase average customer value by 25 per cent and sometimes much more, a huge prize. Customer loyalty and staff loyalty go together as a company's contact with customers is via staff. Satisfied long-term employees lead to more loyal and thus more valuable long-term customers.

Finally, Reichheld stressed the value of investor loyalty, a much neglected factor given the high rates of stock turnover (Chapter 4). He praised the long-term investor policies of Warren Buffett and the stability given to the companies involved enabling them to conduct more profitable long-term business.

Reichheld's thesis is a compelling one that has been seriously neglected by companies and advisers. A reappraisal is in order.

Securing employee loyalty

Companies and their investors benefit from staff loyalty, but securing it under ever-increasing global competition without being able to promise job security in return poses a problem. Overcoming it involves recognizing that there are two considerations which employees value most in today's changed employment conditions. Firstly, help in maintaining their general employability skills so that if their company has to let them go they can get a good job elsewhere. Secondly, having decent-value, transferable pension arrangements (Chapter 5). Companies recognizing and providing these reasonable terms will secure the loyalty and better performance of all employees whether it can employ them for shorter or longer periods. The ability of such companies to attract the best people with the best performance is clearly also in shareholders' interests.

Well-governed companies are worth more

The evidence that companies which adopt the 'enlightened shareholder' approach are more successful at maximizing their shareholders' long-term value is reinforced by equally important evidence that shareholders also benefit significantly from superior corporate governance. In both Britain and the United States many, perhaps even most, managements have regarded pressures to change corporate governance standards as at best a fad and at worst a time-consuming nuisance, distracting management from its main task of achieving shareholder value, a view not absent from the Hampel Committee deliberations. It is therefore useful to consider the indicative evidence from a minor British study and the much stronger evidence from two major US studies, that good governance is a profitable investment in its own right.

The British evidence

The British evidence comes from a May 1997 report by Manifest, a consultancy which advises institutional investors how to vote at company annual general meetings.[11] The study found that poor share price and dividend performance in Britain's largest public companies tend to be associated with reluctance to implement corporate best practice guidelines as set out in the Cadbury and Greenbury reports (the Hampel Report was not public at the time of the analysis). The corporate governance weaknesses identified with poorer shareholder performance included directors on contracts longer than one year, and higher than average fees to accountants for consultancy as opposed to audit work. To reach these conclusions, Manifest examined the UK's then 140 largest public companies which, according to a London Business School Risk Management Service, had achieved in aggregate a 17 per cent total shareholder return in 1996. Manifest concentrated on the thirty-five lowest quartile performances and found that 74 per cent of them had directors' contracts in excess of one year. (In contrast, a separate review of 8,000 directors' contracts in the 140 companies investigated reassuringly revealed that 75 per cent were for one year or less as recommended by Greenbury.) Equally, the same companies had failed to implement other best practice recommendations. The Manifest analysis is not conclusive, merely indicative, but it is useful in a critical area where objective research is rare. For superior and more far-ranging analyses one must turn to America.

The American evidence

The absentee ownership weakness of Anglo-American capitalism has been commented on extensively in earlier chapters. Yet where there are major influential shareholders, or more importantly, a controlling shareholder, they frequently affect share prices for good or ill. Prices are higher where managements are held accountable in the general interest of all shareholders, and lower where influence tolerates inefficiencies or where there is exploitation. These consequences have always been known but seldom quantified. New research by a group of American economists published in late 1999 sheds light on this important problem.[12] Their study is a comprehensive one of nearly 400 companies in twenty-seven developed countries. They find that the better investors are protected anywhere, the higher the value they put on assets, but that when shareholders have more power than their investment entitles them to, it is usually harmful to the company concerned and thus to all the other shareholders, often a majority. Clearly effective corporate governance, if it can be achieved, is one of the most obvious and sensible ways of avoiding the exploitation and thus achieving the enhancement of shareholder values which are the concerns of the NBER paper.

The second US paper, by McKinsey, one of the leading international management consulting firms, is one of the best investigations to date.[13] It directly addresses the worth of good corporate governance. The study opens with a quotation from a sceptical CEO of a Fortune 500 company to the effect that board governance is a fad kept alive by consultants and academics. He wanted evidence that it could matter to shareholders, and the authors set out to provide it. Working with Institutional Investors Inc., McKinsey found that good governance could be quantified and was significant.

McKinsey began by surveying fifty major investors from the Institutional Investors Institute with \$840bn under management and sixty-nine CEOs and top executives from Fortune 1000 companies with average sales of \$2.3bn, a credible sample of tough-minded business-people. The survey was supplemented by interviews.

For the survey purpose well-governed companies were defined as having as a minimum:

- a clear majority of outsiders on the board;
- truly independent directors with no management ties;
- directors with significant stock holdings and paid to a large extent in stock;
- directors who are formally evaluated; and
- boards that are responsive to investor requests.

These are quite searching governance requirements.

The authors made five significant findings. First, 50 per cent of participants would both pay more for the stock of companies passing the five-point governance test, and they were willing to quantify it. A further 16 per cent would pay more, but were unable to quantify. But for two-thirds of investors to be willing to pay more, corporate boards should take notice. Second, the extra premium they would pay averaged 11 per cent (16 per cent for those who would pay more) – a significant sum, equivalent to a permanent 11 per cent increase in earnings. This is too large a potential premium to ignore. A third important and logical finding was that investors with low portfolio turnovers would pay more (12 per cent) than with high (7 per cent), i.e. well-governed companies are worth more to longer-term investors.

A fourth finding was that the 60 per cent of investors willing to pay more for governance described themselves as 'value' investors, compared with only 42 per cent of those unwilling to pay more. Growth investors going for companies with high P/E ratios valued good governance less, believing they were either backing exceptional management or that the industry was growing fast.

Fifth, investors who managed funds for wealthy individuals, foundations and public sector pension funds were willing to pay more for good governance than those running corporate pension funds. The authors speculate that the latter group are less willing to be confrontational with corporate boards, which is the case in Britain (see Chapters 2 and 4).

Three reasons were identified why investors would pay more for good governance:

1. because well-governed firms will perform better long term;
2. because risks are expected to be lower (less likely to happen and more quickly rectified when they do); and
3. because even if it is only a fad firms perceived to be well governed will be more highly rated.

Good governance was seen to matter to investors more in a crisis, more in declining industries reluctant to release cash flows for investment elsewhere, and more where product markets were not sufficiently competitive.

Some 67 per cent of CEOs also valued good governance, and they were willing to pay an even higher premium than investors (24 per cent) for the stock of well-governed companies. For some it was because such companies could handle crises better. Even poorly performing companies with good governance were seen to have a better future than those without since good governance structures could not be implemented quickly but were the patient fruit of years.

To sum up, the authors claim, with reasonable justification, that there were solid grounds for believing in the value of good governance, and to a significant extent. They made two other important comments. First, their survey was only a rough attempt at quantification. Second, governance deserved to be on the priority list for senior management, but it will not often be one of the very top items which will nearly always include strategy, cash flow, management quality, competitive position and cost control. Nevertheless, the only relevant question is whether good governance is worth the cost of achieving it. The authors' quantification of the potential rewards, however, are sufficiently high against the modest costs involved to justify putting it on the agenda of any public company board with major room for governance improvement. There cannot be many policy options which might add 11 per cent plus to share values at any cost never mind a relatively modest one.

Combined insights

Three final points stand out. First, the McKinsey research does not stand alone: the authors quote from six other supporting research studies. Second, the significant gains which they have quantified relate only to the best of *conventional* corporate governance and not the further potential of the governance approach to be outlined below (Chapter 8) which directly addresses the many disabling weaknesses set out in Chapters 2–5. Third, it does not include the wider long-term benefits accruing to shareholders from companies which take account of the wider interests of all the other essential contributors to corporate success. These points, taken together, strongly suggest that well-conceived corporate governance can make a major contribution to long-term corporate success.

CHAPTER 7

An Evaluation of Previously Proposed Remedies

On so important a topic as corporate governance there have been many major British and US reports, investigations, books and articles since the early 1990s putting forward proposals for reform. Despite the changes recommended, their overall impact has been relatively small. The major weaknesses identified in Part II, particularly absentee ownership, persist.

The proposals are considered in four groupings. First are the significant contributions of the main 'official' inquiries (Cadbury, Greenbury, Hampel, etc.). Second are the more advanced proposals, from the Centre for Tomorrow's Company, etc., and a number of prominent writers. Third are the more radical 'stakeholder' views of Will Hutton, John Kay and Aubrey Silberston. Fourth are the key views and proposals of Robert Monks, his profound analysis of current governance ills, and his most innovative and appealing remedial practical proposals.

The proposals are evaluated against the both identified weaknesses and the criteria of Chapter 6.

Mainstream business proposals

The Cadbury Report (1992)

A committee was set up under Sir Adrian Cadbury in 1991 by the London Stock Exchange and accounting institutions in response to some major corporate scandals and the sudden failure of certain prominent companies despite passing their annual audits. Both developments had caused considerable public disquiet. A third concern was widespread unease over high and growing levels of executive remuneration. Taken together it was felt British corporate governance standards were inadequate and needed strengthening. The Committee was asked to report on the *financial* aspects of governance, including:

- the responsibilities of executive and non-executive directors;
- the case for board audit committees, and their composition and remit;
- the principal responsibilities of auditors; and
- links between shareholders, boards and auditors.

The Committee, which reported at the end of 1992 after wide soundings, accepted that boards needed the freedom to drive their companies forward but within a framework of effective accountability. Most of the recommendations were sensible, unexceptionable and well received. These included:

- the general desirability of separating the chairman and CEO roles;
- full board involvement in a formal process to select non-executive directors;
- forming board audit, remuneration and nomination committees of mainly non-executive directors;
- a general strengthening of auditing, rotating audit partners but not their firms; and
- listing progress on the above in annual reports (what the Hampel Report later considered to be mere 'box-ticking').

The most important emphasis was the need for strong, independent, non-executive directors considered to have the pivotal role in ensuring effective governance. The investment institutions were expected to take 'a positive interest in the composition of boards of directors . . . and . . . *the appointment of a core of non-executive directors of the necessary calibre, experience and independence*' (my italics). Thus the first major official report strongly endorsed the need for truly independent non-executive directors, chosen with institutional shareholders' involvement. The institutions supported the idea in general principle but in practice did nothing about it. They have the same attitude eight years later. The system has continued with existing board members choosing their successors because the institutions will not get involved. Absentee ownership and lack of effective accountability perforce continue.

The importance of the Cadbury Report is not in doubt. It confirmed that shareholders (particularly the institutions) have important obligations, even if it failed to secure compliance. It greatly strengthened the powers of non-executive directors on audit and remuneration, although disquiet persists on auditors' full independence from managements. Perversely, directors' remuneration has grown faster since remuneration committees of non-executives were universally accepted (Chapter 1). Nomination committees are less common than the other two, but their influence has been beneficial with fewer cosy appointments. But there is still insufficient independence involved in choosing directors to ensure shareholder interests prevail. Full independence and hence unquestioned legitimacy have not yet been established. However, and increasingly, corporate governance has been established as a necessary and legitimate corporate requirement. All boards must pay much more than lip service to it. And every board or corporate crisis ensures that governance is taken more seriously. It is the main achievement of the Cadbury Committee that there can be no going back to the old complacent ways, even if very much more remains to be done. As the first official committee it made a good start and achieved more than its successors.

The Greenbury Report (1995)

The next official corporate governance report was that of the committee chaired by Sir Richard Greenbury, chairman of Marks & Spencer. It was set up at the CBI's instigation to address the increasingly vexed subject of directors' remuneration in major quoted companies, a matter which concerned the then Conservative government as it now does New Labour. (Faced with serious public disquiet, both governments prefer shareholders to address the problems despite the obvious fact that they have little influence.) The catalyst for the investigation was the particular disquiet over rewards to senior managements in the recently privatised utility companies whose pay, bonuses and pensions had increased four- to six-fold despite the largely non-competitive markets in which they operated. A further concern (unchanged to the present) was large termination payments to CEOs dismissed for underperformance or even failure.

This Committee mainly comprised the chairmen/CEOs of some of Britain's largest companies, a few institutional investors, and the head of the Institute of Directors (IoD). The composition was widely criticized on the grounds that senior businessmen were being asked to judge their own and their peers' rewards, with few independent members to challenge them. In fact the Committee produced a hard-hitting report, and in only six months.

The key principles in the Report were:

- eliminating conflicts of interest by delegating executive compensation to independent non-executive directors;
- linking rewards to individual and corporate performance;
- aligning interests of executive directors and shareholders;
- providing full remuneration disclosure on individual directors; and
- requiring an annual report on progress.

The Report expanded these principles with specific recommendations, including:

- the remuneration committee to be solely non-executive directors;
- the committee to publish its guidelines annually;
- the full disclosure of all remuneration, including pension provision;
- the avoidance of self-ratcheting pay comparisons with peer companies;
- independent remuneration advice;

- long-term incentive (LTI) schemes with challenging criteria linked to shareholder performance for a minimum of three years;
- encouragement for directors to hold shares after receiving share options; and
- ensuring directors' remuneration was consistent and fair in relation to employees.

The proposals were well received and acted upon with four important exceptions. First, independent advice for remuneration committees is rare. Second, little has happened to ensure shares are held long term. Third, directors' remuneration has not been linked to that of employees. Fourth, there was strong senior management opposition to the fullest pension cost disclosure (see Chapter 2) resulting in two options. (The less full disclosure option has been chosen by many companies – with little criticism from investment institutions.) Avoidance of change will always occur when reforms are proposed unless entities exist to hold directors accountable. Hence an admirable and radical report has failed to achieve its objective. Senior director remuneration for the top 100 companies increased 45 per cent in the year after the report and has gone on rising steeply since. The three-year LTI minimum is the effective maximum.

Part of the reason for failure was that the Committee's terms of reference were to identify 'good practice'. But with absentee ownership and a lack of accountability 'good practice' cannot identify an acceptable answer if most companies follow the same practices which caused the inquiry to be set up. Only committees of mainly disinterested members with an appropriately wide brief can produce not only a good report (and Greenbury passed that test) but one with effective proposals for turning it into reality.

The Myners Report (1995/6)

At government initiative a joint senior City/industry group was set up under Paul Myners, chairman of a major fund manager, Gartmore. Its purpose was to suggest practical ways to improve industry/investment institutional relationships for 'long-term investment and development', thus implicitly acknowledging short-term pressures. It described short-termism as a destructive and sterile debate, but accepted much more could be done to develop 'a winning long-term partnership'. It advocated that a 'model investor' should:

- be more open in discussing strategy and management;
- state its own investment objectives clearly;
- be active in corporate governance (voting, etc);
- improve staff training; and
- prepare well for corporate meetings.

In turn, a model company should:

- make annual strategic presentations to institutions and analysts focusing on the long term;
- improve AGMs and communications; and
- set out a clear remuneration policy and discuss it openly with shareholders.

Pension fund trustees should:

- set long-term goals for their fund managers; and
- set sufficiently long-term objectives to encourage fund managers to back their long-term judgement.

These were commendable recommendations but did not address the major difficulties and conflicts of interest identified earlier (Chapters 2–5). The report implicitly assumed that long-term *holding* of shares was the same as being a long-term *owner*.

The report criticized the failure to link executive remuneration to long-term performance, and urged three- to five-year objectives and investor willingness to take action when dissatisfied. It noted that twenty years of share options had not led to widespread share ownership by executives. It was even harder on pension fund trustees for lacking the necessary investment expertise to set fund managers' targets. Over-reliance on short-term fund league tables was criticised, as was the failure to instruct fund managers on how to vote on contentious issues. Corporate managements were criticized for often having poor shareholder relationships.

Finally, the report considered a model investor would be 'very much . . . an investor on behalf of the beneficial owners', i.e. a long-term investor with a relatively low portfolio turnover. The Committee believed its recommendations represented best current practice and would lead to the creation of winning long-term partnerships between companies and owners.

It was a sensible report, but it remains largely an aspiration. The unresolved systemic weaknesses were not fully identified or addressed. Hence relationships are little changed five years later.

The Hampel Report (1998)

A committee was set up at the end of 1995 at the behest of the Stock Exchange under the chairman of ICI, Sir Ronnie Hampel. Its membership was also drawn mainly from the senior ranks of industry, plus representatives from the CBI, the investment institutions' associations, etc. It was to review what had happened since the Cadbury Report, to promote the highest standards of governance to protect investors and company regulators, to review the functions and effectiveness of executive and non-executive directors, and to address the role of auditors and shareholders. It was to be done in the context of restricting the regulatory burden on companies and to substitute principles for detail wherever possible.

The Committee saw its role as a consolidatory one (its proposals and those of the earlier committees became the Stock Exchange's 'Combined Code' in 1998). It did not consider whether there were unresolved major governance weaknesses. Its tone from the outset was that governance activity had become excessive and needed reining back. The annual corporate reports on how well its predecessors' require-ments were being met were said to be concentrating on the letter rather than the spirit of the intentions, and should be changed.

The Committee held that wealth creation was the overwhelming duty of corporate boards and that governance accountability require-ments were a rather secondary matter because 'public companies are now amongst the most accountable organisations in society'. The clear inference was that accountability could handicap wealth creation and should therefore be constrained. There was little acknowledgement that managements' and shareholders' interests could and frequently did diverge, e.g. over justified remuneration. There were no proposals for greater shareholder involvement. The Myners Report with its exhortatory proposals was commended as covering most of what was necessary, yet there was no discussion or even awareness that its worthy proposals largely remained to be implemented. The Report held that it was up to institutions to exercise their votes. The self-perpetuating nature of the corporate boards, with all major powers centred on it (Figure 2 and Chapter 2), the disabling conflicts of interest of investment institutions, absentee ownership, etc., received little comment.

The justification for the Committee's satisfaction with the status quo was that it fully accepted the central role of directors in directing and controlling companies 'linked to the role of shareholders [agreed], *since they appoint the directors*' (my italics). As set out in Chapter 1, this traditional view, while nominally true, is so far from reality that it undermines the whole basis of the Hampel Report. It is the fault of shareholders not directors that shareholders take no part in selecting directors and almost never fail to endorse a board's candidate unanimously, but that does not make it an independent process of shareholder control. The Committee's view was in marked contrast to the Cadbury Report. It contradicted the views of nearly all governance experts in Britain and America in the last decade, and the views of Britain's own leading journals (*The Times*, *The Financial Times* and *The Economist*).

The Hampel Report, however, made a number of important points:

- directors retiring early should explain their reasons for leaving;
- corporate governance had a neglected contribution to make to national efficiency and prosperity;
- the Myners Report's recommendations for closer contact between boards and institutional shareholders were to be encouraged;
- shareholder primacy should be pursued in the context of developing and sustaining stakeholder relationships;
- there should be a more formal procedure for board appointments; and
- companies should have regard to broader public acceptability of their conduct.

I agree with them all. They showed vision, perception and sensibility to widespread public misgivings. But I regret the failure to recognize the systemic weaknesses which so handicap the governance system and largely prevent the desirable recommendations of all the main official inquiries from Cadbury to Hampel from having major effect. Little progress is possible until the systemic weaknesses are directly add-ressed.

More advanced proposals

Some of the more interesting of the more advanced proposals are briefly set out below. They are not particularly radical and so could be acceptable to mainstream business opinion. Indeed a number of them have been implemented by some major companies.

The Centre for Tomorrow's Company

The views of this policy institute were set out at length and commended in the previous chapter. The essence of the Centre's philosophy is that while shareholder primacy must remain, if we are to have more world-class companies their boards must also meet the long-term expectations of all the main corporate participants. (The word 'stakeholders' is usually avoided because of its political associ-ations.) It recognizes that corporate success is a *joint* product of all participants, hence companies succeed best when they have an 'inclusive' approach to and regard for the interests of the employees, customers, communities, etc., involved. Companies with this ap-proach have the best chance of creating long-term sustainable value. Accordingly, the Centre urges a wider range of measures for judging companies than the necessary but not sufficient financial ones.

The Centre, whose membership includes many of Britain's most successful companies, is advocating an approach compatible with all four official reports, albeit with greater emphasis on the need for 'in-clusiveness'.

Jonathan Charkham

Jonathan Charkham – businessman, lawyer, writer, member of the Cadbury Committee and a former industrial adviser to the Governor of

the Bank of England – has been one of the most influential com-
mentators on corporate governance in the last decade. He is the author
of the best survey of comparative corporate governance of the five main
industrial countries.[1]

He has mainly concentrated on analysis rather than remedies but
has clearly articulated the principles to which effective solutions to
governance weaknesses should conform. He argues that the prime test
of a corporate governance system is its ability to combine 'dynamism'
(wealth creation) and accountability, recognizing that accountability
covers standards of behaviour as well as competence. He sees a main
weakness of Anglo-American capitalism as short-termism imposed by
financial market pressures, and the seeking of immediate share value
enhancement despite potential long-term harm to companies and all
who depend on them. The cause is due to neglect of ownership duties
which only investment institutions can remedy by providing or
procuring it on a sustainable long-term basis, otherwise management
interests can diverge from those of owners.

In his latest book, which he has co-authored with Anne Simpson,
most of the text is devoted to analysing the composition, character and
views of all the many shareholder entities, making it an important
reference book.[2] The authors also set out a proposed remedy for more
effectively discharging the vital ownership responsibilities. They urge
'significant owners' (defined as those who own 0.5 per cent or £25m
worth of shares), say the top twenty shareholders per quoted company,
to accept an 'enhanced duty of care', i.e. to exercise ownership
responsibilities, especially voting, on the principle that if it is not their
duty whose else could it be? Should it prove necessary, shares which
were voted could qualify for a slightly higher dividend to compensate
for efforts on behalf of all shareholders. (Should this not come to pass
the authors favour at least the right of shareholders to vote for a two-tier
board, but see it as an inferior substitute for their main proposal, since
shareholders would still need to be active.)

The approach is a sound one which would address many of the main
governance weaknesses. But given the main reinforcing and disabling
conflicts of interest identified earlier, it is difficult to see how it would
come to pass. No laws need to be changed so it could have been
implemented by now. I doubt if it can or will be taken up until the
conflicts of interest, etc., are resolved (see the catalytic proposals in

Chapter 8) but if they are it is certainly a candidate for shareholder response.

John Plender

John Plender, a *Financial Times* leader writer and regular broadcaster, is another influential governance commentator. His 1997 book *A Stake in the Future*[3] is a penetrating centre-left assessment of current British capitalism. It is an optimistic book that argues strongly for market values tempered by a humane appreciation that prosperity is the joint product of all business participants. To overcome the widespread dissatisfaction with much of current British capitalism (Chapter 1) he outlines the principles to be followed in seeking remedies. First, the behaviour of markets needs to be tempered by *self-imposed* social and ethical constraints. The values of loyalty and trust within companies foster wealth creation and contribute to competitive advantage, whereas fear (of unemployment, poor pensions, etc.) does the opposite. Next, he strongly urges the need to rethink the provision of occupational pensions to ensure employees share the rewards of capitalism and not just its risks. Last, he stresses the need for the big investment institutions to achieve a constructive relationship with the companies in which they invest on behalf of the many millions of disenfranchised beneficial owners. These are principles with wide relevance and resonance (see Chapters 5, 6 and 8).

Charles M. Elson

Charles Elson is a widely published American expert on management remuneration and directors' compensation, and a professor at the Stetson University Law School in Florida. He is no mere academic commentator since he was responsible for ousting the colourful exponent of repeated mass redundancies, Al 'Chainsaw' Dunlap.[4] Elson was brought on to the board of Sunbeam by Dunlap as a governance expert and shareholder activist. In mid-1998 when Dunlap was evasive with directors on the exact decline in second-quarter sales figures, and refused repeated requests for information, Elson secured his dismissal within days.

The main reason for mentioning Elson, however, is his work on the best form of board remuneration in the light of the widespread Anglo-American concern that executive remuneration is often excessive. His proposals were aptly summarized in a letter to *The Financial Times* commenting on the Greenbury Report.[5] He felt the Greenbury proposals could not solve the mismatch between excessive remuneration and poor performance since it neglected the bargaining process between directors. As senior managers largely appoint non-executives, excessive remuneration results from passive boards beholden to their appointers. They have little incentive for spirited negotiation. To overcome this Elson proposed to link non-executives to shareholder interests by paying them largely in company shares *which could not be sold during their term of office*. Once non-executives had been in office a few years they would have a substantial investment and a powerful financial incentive to act more independently. He cited extensive evidence for his proposal which has led to it being increasingly taken up by American companies. (This is consistent with the findings of the Institute of Directors and A. P. Williams set out in Chapter 1 – that there is a positive correlation between high levels of director share ownership and high levels of performance, and the converse.) These are important and encouraging findings for corporate governance improvement. The proposed reform is fully compatible with the independent appointment of non-executive directors as well as being attractive in its own right (see Chapter 8). In June 2000 Pilkington pioneered it in Britain.

Radical stakedholder proposals

Two radical British proposals are considered next, which propose corporate accountability to wider groups than shareholders. While I am opposed to the views, they raise some valid concerns which I believe are better met in other ways.

Will Hutton

The author of a highly successful 1995 book,[6] Will Hutton, journalist, broadcaster and now director of the Industrial Society, is one of the leading advocates of a radical stakeholder approach to political, economic and corporate life. I have considered only his views on corporate governance from his major book and two others.[7] I set out my understanding of his views with my comments in square brackets.

1. There is a need for some long-term shareholder commitment best achieved by groups of core institutional shareholders with board representation and a secretariat. [I broadly agree in principle.]
2. Voting rights might be limited to institutional shareholders with board responsibilities thus legally linking ownership to duties. [While I also seek some committed owners and independent non-executive directors, I strongly disagree with non-voting shares as wrong in principle and unnecessary in practice. All shareholders are entitled to votes – the City fought a long campaign to get rid of non-voting shares. The need is to make voting a worthwhile activity on behalf of all shareholders.]
3. Takeovers should be made harder. [As takeovers and mergers are often wasteful and unsuccessful (Chapter 3), the need is to address conflicts of interests between shareholders and managements and to make decision taking more objective by having independently advised, independent non-executive directors.]
4. Audit needs to be regulated in the public interest, with auditors having to be licensed. [The concern of auditors' conflict of interest is best addressed by auditors being in separate firms from their consulting colleagues as is beginning to happen – see Chapter 2.]
5. There should be an upper limit on advisers' fees. [The remedy would be unworkable. Independent non-executive directors, independently advised is the better way.]
6. Narrowly interpreted shareholder interests overwhelm wider stakeholder interests, frequently to the detriment of all concerned and should be replaced by a stakeholders' corporate objective to ensure national efficiency and social cohesiveness.

This last point, the central core of Will Hutton's views, deserves a fuller comment. For all the reasons set out in the previous chapter I reject the stakeholder criteria as completely unworkable and not in the long-run interest even of stakeholders. Shareholder primacy must prevail, but as set out at length, wise and successful companies pay due attention to the interests of all key participants, who, as the evidence shows, benefit far more than under any other conceivable arrangement. The dilemma of shareholder versus stakeholder interests is a false one. Such corporate wisdom can only be copied not legislated for. But if companies can be made accountable to the interests of their individual and beneficial shareholders, they are much more likely to look after the interests of all the other participants as they share the same general long-term interests (Chapter 6).

Nowhere does Will Hutton advocate stakeholder board representation. Rather the difference between us is that I am optimistic that corporate governance is capable of effective reform with only modest government catalytic actions. The rest could then safely be left to market forces (Chapter 8). This approach would better meet his underlying concerns.

John Kay and Aubrey Silberston

The most serious of all stakeholder proposals was put forward in 1995 by the well-regarded academic economists John Kay and Aubrey Silberston.[8] (John Kay is also the founder of a major economic consultancy.) The most significant part of the wide-ranging article was the examination of the rights of ownership. It concluded that public companies neither are nor can be effectively owned by shareholders, and that this is anyway undesirable. The authors prefer to view companies as social institutions. Accordingly, they proposed an alternative 'the trustee model of corporate governance'. Instead of being responsible to shareholders, directors would enhance corporate asset values and balance fairly the claims of all stakeholders. Businesses were seen as a nexus of long-established trust relationships. (I fully agree but draw different conclusions – see Chapters 6 and 8.) In a private discussion I learnt that the trustee role would fall primarily on three non-executive directors and a non-executive chairman. A *Financial Times* editorial[9] commended the approach for overcoming non-executive directors having to be both players and referees (the role is inescapable – see Chapter 8). The authors believed their model avoided non-executives being 'a shareholder spy in the boardroom' (not a role of which they are commonly accused – to be criticized for being the tool of executives would be more usual). German and Japanese directors were seen as effectively 'trustee directors' – but the now widely perceived failure in those nations' corporate governance was their neglect of reasonable shareholder priorities, a matter now being addressed urgently in Germany and slowly in Japan.

The authors have given little thought to the trustee directors' objectives other than the vague promotion of the company's business and balancing the claims of all stakeholders. The abandonment of shareholder primacy would mean almost any board decision could be justified under the trustee model. What would happen when stakeholder priorities clashed, as they surely will? There is an unbridgeable gap between recognizing and responding to legitimate stakeholder interests under long-term shareholder primacy and abandoning such primacy (Chapter 6). Further, shareholder primacy is the major guarantor of nearly all private and occupational pensions, a huge and unmentioned stakeholder interest which would be imperilled. The authors criticize the traditional governance system for short-term behaviour, particularly over too many poor-value takeovers and mergers, and for not preventing excessive executive remuneration. The fault, however, is not the aim of shareholder primacy, but its neglect due to absentee ownership and the neutering of institutional shareholders and fund managers, with all major powers falling by default on executive directors (see Figure 2 and Chapters 1 and 2).

The authors have moved to the trustee model, having concluded that the shareholder model is incapable of reform, a view I emphatically reject (Chapter 8). They have given up too soon. They assumed no changes would be possible to provide independent shareholder directors who can take the long-term view, hold managements accountable and have the capability of ensuring successful co-operation with all the key participants upon whom corporate success depends.

The authors have given little thought as to how trustee directors would be appointed. If not by shareholders only, how are votes to be given to stakeholders, which ones, and in what proportions? Further, their model is incapable of voluntary introduction because neither individual nor institutional shareholders would forfeit the right at least to ratify the appointment of directors, and no government would dare to impose it. Stock markets would collapse. Only owners, whose capital is at risk, can choose directors. The solution is not to abandon the present system of shareholder primacy but to reform it, to have capable, fully independent non-executive directors sustained by sufficient active, knowledgeable and committed owners, or entities able to provide the equivalent – the heart of my own proposals. But even if proposals along these lines are not implemented, there is no possibility of introducing the trustee model whatever the shortcomings of the present system.

John Kay has since modified his views. He frankly acknowledges the big difficulty for the advocates of stakeholding, namely suggesting achievable, practicable remedies for perceived ills. Instead, he settles for the reality that stakeholding is essentially about attitudes, about companies acknowledging a wider range of responsibilities than shareholder value,[10] the essential philosophy of most long-term successful companies (Chapter 6). The valid part of stakeholding is these values, rather than the usually flawed detailed proposals of its proponents. The forceful advocacy of these values is John Kay's major and lasting contribution to governance improvement.

Robert Monks's proposals

Monks's background

Robert Monks is America's most prominent and effective shareholder and corporate governance activist. He is also a prominent lawyer, businessman and a former US Department of Labor pensions fund regulator. With his American shareholder activist company LENS having joint ventures with the major British fund manager Hermes, he is also the leading international activist as corporate governance is more advanced in Britain than elsewhere. Continuing his partnership with Hermes, the focus is now being extended to Western Europe.

Robert Monks was the first to identify corporate directors, particularly the non-executives, as the pivotal balance between the interests of managements and their shareholders.

Corporate activity

In 1985, Robert Monks set up Institutional Shareholder Services (ISS), a private sector firm, to advise American institutional investors on voting opportunities and responsibilities, recognizing the huge economies from sharing analysis and knowledge. (It is rare for an American institution to own more than a 0.5 per cent interest in the top 500 companies.) In 1992, he established LENS, a special-purpose activist investment partnership that invests its own and its clients' money in a small number of medium to very large underperforming companies. The chosen name indicates LENS's focus on identifying and closing the governance gap in underperforming companies. LENS has achieved a 3–4 per cent outperformance against the S & P 500 index by focusing on a very small number of underperforming mega companies (Sears Roebuck, American Express, Eastman Kodak, etc.) where its well-publicized catalytic intervention has led to major improvements. (This performance is being repeated in the LENS–Hermes British partnership.) Instead of spotting 'winners', LENS has concentrated on 'losers' whose underperformance it could help to raise. It has thus proved Monks's lifelong philosophy that companies having independent, informed, motivated and empowered owners are worth more than those without (see Chapter 6).

The LENS example has not been widely followed partly because of the 'free-rider' problem. (As an influential but very small shareholder over 99 per cent of the large gains LENS helped to achieve accrued to other passive investors.) Even more important are the serious conflicts of interest (fear of antagonizing present or potential clients, unwillingness to risk the reputation of hostility to managements, etc.) which inhibit most institutional investors (Chapter 2). Further, institutions lack senior people with the necessary aptitude, fortitude and specialized experience.

Anglo-American activists deserve the full commendation of all other shareholders whom they benefit at no cost, but there will never be enough of them to provide an universal remedy for ineffective governance. Their contribution is significant but transient. Permanent remedies for quoted companies in general require other wider approaches. It was with this in mind that Robert Monks, usually with his LENS partner Nell Minow, has written numerous influential books and countless articles over the last decade, culminating in his most recent and important book,[11] the most thorough and enlightening history of the modern corporation, and a profound analysis of its current ills. Although based on American corporations, its major insights are of universal application. The final chapter, the 'Epilogue', contains the main proposal to which no brief summary can do justice.

An outline of the main proposal

The proposal emerges from a forecast of what may evolve in America and then Britain in the next decade as the pressures for major corporate governance reform become irresistible. Monks describes how a new intermediary investment institution may emerge from the governance momentum of the 1990s. During this era, as corporate power in the face of global mega companies expands beyond the scope and largely beyond the restraining power of nation states, it would become increasingly recognised that management and corporate accountability were becoming alarmingly weaker still. Increasingly, institutional shareholders would recognise that only their combined latent power would suffice to provide accountability. Governments were increasingly ineffective and unwilling to act. ('These matters should be left to shareholders in a free market.') Sufficient American corporations would be increasingly seen as having undue political influence, as breaking the law, e.g. bribery in defence contracts, as hiding the health and environmental damage they cause, and as having CEOs and senior managements abusing their power – e.g. to secure excessive remuneration.

The author, from an imagined 2010 perspective, describes a catalytic Supreme Court judgment that pension fund trustees and other fiduciaries must act *solely* in their beneficiaries' interests for the *exclusive purpose* of providing them with benefits. Further and crucially, *fiduciaries may need to step aside, at least temporarily, where there is a substantial conflict of interest.* This landmark ruling set a permanent federal standard of ownership. At a stroke the conflict of interests of pension fund trustees, insurance companies, fund managers (even company directors) were effectively outlawed, although it would take some years for this to become fully apparent and put into effect.

Optimizing long-term value for beneficiaries had to be the *sole* priority for pension fund trustees – anything else was a breach of trust. The same applied to insurance companies and fund managers. The choice was clear, the management appointed trustees of pension funds had to cease entirely to be guided by or favour management in discharging their duties. The traditional multi-service fiduciary institutions had to give up either their fiduciary work, or all the rest. All concerned took the easier course, and a new institution, the Special Purpose Trust Company (SPTC) was born, first in the United States, but soon afterwards in Britain and Canada. Its sole function was to act as owner with respect to the securities held in the investment portfolios of its institutional clients, i.e. to safeguard beneficiaries' interests by voting on all issues before company meetings including the election of directors.

A brief summary cannot set out the full probable effects of this new institution but it would be likely to provide a truly 'new governance' with real and continuous corporate *and* institutional accountability. The old order whereby 'co-operative' financial institutions received lucrative contracts in return for mute compliance would end. It would be reinforced, in response to a predicted presidential directive, by a US government declaration that *'the existence of independent and informed owners in the governance of public companies is in the public interest'*. The declaration would be followed by a summary of existing standards concerning the fiduciary duties of owners, and an intergovernmental agency group formed to ensure enforcement of the *existing* law in a consistent manner. The law would not be changed, but the government would in future enforce a strict and universal compliance. This environment would naturally create a market for the SPTCs which would provide a channel for this new form of fiduciary capitalism.

The SPTCs' existence and activities would be based on a simple, overriding dictum: *in a free society you cannot have power without accountability.* They would begin by proposing resolutions at AGMs, for a 'corporate civility code' to ensure American companies no longer continued the abuses outlined above. The all-powerful watchdog, the Securities and Exchange Commission (SEC), would require such resolutions to be put to AGMs where they would attract strong shareholder support. Managements could not fail to obey laws fully, nor damage health and the environment covertly, nor use shareholder funds for self-serving political lobbying (e.g. to avoid having to disclose the true costs of the huge and existing stock options – frequently 10 per cent plus of all American shares).

Gradually senior managements, pension fund trustees, fund managers, etc., would realize they could no longer act with serious conflicts of interest, and increasingly they would turn to SPTCs to discharge independently the voting and other ownership duties (full discretion) in the sole and exclusive interests of beneficiaries. It would be the only safe, sensible and effective way in litigious America of avoiding unacceptable personal risks to directors, trustees, etc. The policy guideline to SPTCs would be to realize the gains from ownership involvement and to affirm the *basic values* of the 100 million plus beneficial owners mainly saving for retirement (see Chapter 6).

SPTCs would function in two sharply different roles. First, they would monitor corporate managements and, if they continued to underperform, would take appropriate remedial action, including eventually changing boards of directors and senior managers. Second, they would provide guidance to managements on the long-term needs of owners, and ensure continuous accountability.

An evaluation

Several points stand out. First, the existing law governing trustees and fiduciaries must eventually be rigorously enforced. Beneficial share-holders and hence government will come to insist upon it.

Second, limited government catalytic actions would be required to break the present governance stalemate, the *systemic* fault which, because of major unavoidable conflicts of interest, the various parties, and particularly the investment institutions and fund managers, cannot resolve themselves (Chapter 2).

Third, once the quite limited government actions have taken place, market solutions to governance problems would take over. The SPTCs would have no monopoly grip on their functions. They would compete vigorously with each other for clients, staff and the provision of relevant competence and expertise. Their income would be determined solely by competitive market forces.

Fourth, without the present existing conflicts of interest, investment institutions and fund managers would be freed to concentrate on their main task of successful investment.

Fifth, there would be an effective discharge of ownership re-sponsibilities in the sole interest of beneficiaries. The proposals would offer the means to secure majority shareholder support on major issues. Even the increasing number of global mega companies would be held accountable if the proposals were taken up on a sufficient scale, and usually without the need either for government intervention or the co-operative intervention of several governments.

Sixth, if state pension funds are to be invested in equities, as looks possible in America, and has already happened elsewhere, insistence upon SPTCs would free governments from controlling large blocs of shares – a very necessary defence of freedom. (The same would apply in Britain if gradually the basic state pension is moved over to a funded basis invested in equities – Chapter 5.)

Seventh, once the fruits of SPTCs' actions became apparent the movement would quickly acquire an unstoppable momentum as all beneficial shareholders would want it as being in their clear interests. Their agents, the investment institutions and ultimately the fund managers, would have to be supportive or lose clients and put their own futures at risk. In fact these agents should welcome the release from present damaging and ultimately unsustainable conflicts of interest. Executive directors would lose many of the powers they have accrued as shareholders relinquished them, but lacking shareholder support, they could not anyway be maintained long term.

Further governance requirements

The SPTC proposal offers major benefits, but there are some further significant governance requirements that would still need to be addressed. First, there are benefits to companies and shareholders from long-term committed owners over and above the monitoring role of SPTCs. Second, truly independent, high-calibre, non-executive directors are needed for both the monitoring and business strategy roles. This is a matter of business expertise rather than the corporate governance expertise of SPTCs. It would be better discharged in part at least by committed relationship investors who, given their business expertise, would be more effective in holding managements accountable. That said, SPTCs would have a useful role in monitoring non-executive directors' performance, as well as that of executive directors. SPTCs would nearly always command the majority vote and have the final say, as they should.

In sum, the SPTC proposal is the most important corporate governance proposal put forward to date. It offers a major improvement in holding managements accountable and protecting the interests of beneficial owners (and incidentally benefiting individual shareholders). It needs to be supplemented by further complementary measures which are the subject of the next chapter, but it deserves the fullest support from shareholders and government.

CHAPTER 8

A Programme for Reform

The need for an integrated approach

The guidelines

The extensive weaknesses of the present system of corporate governance have been identified plus the gains which could arise from
shareholder primacy combined with effective corporate governance.
Existing proposals for reform have been largely seen to be either
insufficient or incapable of being applied. Taking these analyses into
account, a programme for effective reform can now be developed.

As set out in the Introduction a generally successful system of
corporate governance, i.e. one that is conducive to a humane, confident,
efficient and globally competitive nation, requires three interdependent
preconditions:

- sufficient committed, knowledgeable and active long-term shareholders;
- managements with the preconditions and incentives for long-term
  performance, accountable to shareholders; and
- motivated and valued employees and stakeholders.

In restating these guidelines I would re-emphasize that British capitalism is largely a success story. Overcoming the corporate governance
weaknesses and following the proven approaches considered at length

above (Chapter 6) could further improve corporate and economic performance. They would also go far to restore public confidence in and satisfaction with business.

Interdependent weaknesses

The governance problems arise from the double accountability deficit. Corporate managements are not accountable either to individual shareholders (20 per cent) or to the investment institutions and fund managers, etc. (80 per cent), who are the intermediary agents of the ultimate shareholders. Nor, in turn, are these intermediaries effectively accountable to the ultimate shareholders, the individual beneficiaries who are pension fund members, policyholders, etc. The present situation is not a criticism of corporate managements who have necessarily assumed powers relinquished by shareholders. Indeed it is not anyone's fault. Rather it is the consequence of the way the governance system has slowly evolved over many decades with the decline of powerful controlling shareholders and their replacement by investment institutions. These institutions, for a number of conflict of interest reasons, are seriously inhibited from exercising ownership responsibilities on an effective continuous basis. In sum, there is a *systemic* fault. Nearly all the main governance weaknesses are the consequences of this fault, and as set out at length in Part II, are interdependent and mutually reinforcing. This analysis is summarised in Figure 2, where all major powers are seen to be in the hands of senior management. The stewards have almost become the principals.

The result has been a corporate governance system in which executive directors, and particularly chairmen and CEOs, with so much power concentrated in their own hands, are implicitly, in Robert Monks's memorable phrase 'trustees for the public good'. Given the major conflicts of interest, this is a quite inappropriate responsibility, but it is the inescapable consequence of the systemic fault.

The required key changes

The systemic fault is strongly entrenched. This explains why the remedies of the last decade, useful and welcome though they have been, have not been able to achieve fundamental change. Overcoming the fault requires a number of *simultaneous* interrelated changes, two of which are particularly important. First, it requires the realignment of the long-term interests, risks and rewards of the two principal entities, the *real* shareholders – the 20 per cent individual and the 80 per cent ultimate beneficiary shareholders – and corporate managements.

Second, it requires that there are truly independent non-executive directors, i.e. not chosen by their executive director colleagues who have an unacceptable conflict of interest. This flouts all governance principles, in particular that the 'monitored should choose the monitors'. Instead non-executives must be chosen with the effective involvement of the institutional shareholders. This was a major but stillborn proposal of the Cadbury Report.

These comments are not to impugn existing non-executive directors. But most are uncomfortable and inhibited when it comes to taking difficult decisions against those by whom they were appointed. To take such decisions can also be a very time-consuming process, particularly if it involves a senior dismissal and then finding a competent replacement – more time than many non-executives can easily spare.

The point was put well in a recent hardhitting but not unfair article on the dilemmas that have recently faced the non-executive directors of British Airways, and earlier those of Marks & Spencer. 'The etiquette of the boardroom is to refrain from rocking the boat'.[1] The same people, appointed quite independently and owing nothing to their executive colleagues, would be far more effective. The problem is not the characters and abilities of existing non-executive directors, but the flawed process of their appointment. But with institutional shareholders unwilling to take any part in the selection of non-executive directors, the present unsatisfactory practice will continue until there is an effective external agent of change.

Achieving reform

The acceptance, even the widespread acceptance of this analysis of the contemporary corporate governance *malaise* would be very unlikely to lead any of the main participants to change the status quo. Corporate managements are unlikely voluntarily to relinquish their extensive powers. The investment institutions and fund managers, who largely compete among themselves, lack the means and incentives to overcome their entrenched and paralysing conflicts of interest. The real shareholders, the majority ultimate beneficiaries and the minority individual shareholders, are effectively voiceless. Effective change can come only from government action. All governments in recent years have avoided the issue, saying reforms are the responsibility of shareholders. But, as already stated, shareholders are powerless to overcome the systemic fault. It is government action or the status quo. Fortunately, however, three modest but catalytic government actions could break the deadlock by giving all parties the incentives to provide or procure changes which would overcome the weaknesses, the double accountability deficit. Market forces would then be freed to do the rest.

Catalytic government action

The need is for a programme of initially minimal reform which addresses the identified double accountability deficit in corporate governance in an efficient and practicable way. Given the complexity and importance of the issues, and the difficulty of seeing how reforms would work out in practice, reform should be evolutionary and directed towards encouraging investment institutions and fund managers to evolve their own solutions within the framework of the essential reforms now being proposed. The process would require a corporate governance regulator, one of whose responsibilities would be to review reform progress after three years to determine whether or not the initial reforms needed to be strengthened or modified.

The first requirement, desirably with cross-party agreement, is that the government should affirm that creating an effective shareholder presence in all companies is in the national interest, that there should be no power without accountability, and that this principle should be taken into account by all regulators – the Takeover Panel, the Competition Authority, etc.[2] With the direct and indirect ownership of equities being, with housing, by far the largest personal assets, nothing less than effective accountability should be politically acceptable to any of the main political parties.

The second requirement is that all pension fund trustees and other fiduciaries holding shares must act *solely* in the long-term interests of their beneficiaries and for the *exclusive* purpose of providing them with benefits. (While it can fairly be argued that this is already trust law, it needs to be given specific continuous and strong public emphasis and enforcement to overcome present inertia and conflicts of interest – i.e. to make trustees, fiduciaries, etc pro-active in the sole and exclusive interest of their beneficiaries.)

The third requirement, to give full effect to the first two proposals, is that institutional shareholders should be made accountable for exercising their voting rights in an informed and sensible manner above some sensibly determined minimum holding (e.g. £10m). As votes are an asset (voting shares always have a market premium over non-voting ones), they should be used to further beneficiaries' interests on all occasions. In effect the voting of institutionally held shares would be virtually compulsory.

All three proposals are both necessary and mutually reinforcing. To be compelled to vote without, say, the requirement to do so solely and exclusively in the interests of beneficiaries would, given the inescapably continuing conflicts of interest, be likely to result in institutions taking the line of least resistance. There would be, as at present, an almost automatic vote in support of nearly all corporate management proposals. It would thus give the spurious appearance of democratic accountability while leaving the reality of the double accountability deficit intact.

The purpose of the three proposed government actions is to make both corporate managements and investment institutions effectively accountable to the ultimate shareholders, the millions of beneficiaries who comprise the majority of the working population. They could not, of course, be directly answerable to this huge number of individuals, each with small, individually held beneficial interests in a myriad of companies. The three measures are designed, however, to ensure that trustees and fiduciaries have both the necessity and means to respond *solely and exclusively to their beneficiaries' collective long-term interests.*

An outline programme for reform

Inadequate corporate and institutional accountability is seen to impair efficiency and hence national wealth creation. It also results in the abuse of management remuneration, etc., thus harming the public acceptance of free markets essential to rapid economic growth.

The following proposals which address these issues should form the substance of a government Green Paper for public discussion with the intent of introducing a flexible and effective system for ensuring adequate accountability for UK-based companies. (Overseas based companies pose special problems which could only effectively be addressed by co-operation between governments.)

1. *Widening the regulatory remit*   The existing regulator, the Financial Services Authority, whose remit already covers standards of probity and competence for financial institutions, should have its remit extended to cover the exercise of due diligence by all investment intermediaries in the exercise of their voting rights of all the shares which they hold in UK-based companies either on behalf of third parties or their own shareholders. It is inherently paradoxical that such intermediaries should be tightly regulated as to their honesty and competence in dealing with their investments but under no practical obligation to ensure that shareholder rights in the companies in which they invest are actively, efficiently and continuously discharged, solely and exclusively on behalf of the beneficiaries.

2. *Code of conduct*   The regulatory authority, whether itself, or by establishing a special corporate governance regulator (or 'Ombudsman'), should ensure that the investment institutions would operate within a code of conduct for, say, initially, the top 200 companies. The investment institutions should be charged with the following requirements:

- *Due diligence obligations*   To exercise the obligations of due diligence in the discharge of their governance responsibilities in a demonstrably informed, impartial and responsible manner, solely and exclusively in beneficiaries' interest. (This automatically requires them to exercise voting rights on all occasions since not to do so would be a clear violation of such diligence.) Where the due diligence obligation cannot be effectively discharged directly due to conflicts of interest (a very common case), the obligation would be to procure the exercise of those rights by competent investment intermediaries with no conflicts of interest.
- *Ensuring independent non-executive directors*   To   ensure   that   all

non-executive directors would be independently selected and nominated. (On an initial trial basis existing non-executive directors could act via a nomination committee – a most sensible Cadbury Report proposal – of which they alone were members. They would also need to be advised by an executive search firm of their own choosing with no other connections to the company.)

- *Monitoring non-executive directors* To monitor non-executive directors' activities on the audit, remuneration and nomination committees to ensure they were advised by independent consultants of their own choosing with no other connections to the company or its management. (Thus auditors, whom the audit committee would recommend for annual election to shareholders in place of but after consultation with management, would not also be able to act in the usually far larger role of consultants, because of obvious conflicts of interest, thus ensuring auditors were indisputably fully independent.)

3. *Method of operating* The corporate governance regulator, in the interests of flexibility and the avoidance of bureaucracy, would work primarily by exception. Using the massive amount of research produced by brokers, independent analysts, the press, etc., the first step would be to identify companies with a history of underperformance or apparent management abuse. Then the major institutional shareholders in these companies would be required to show that they had properly exercised due diligence towards these companies to avoid the apparent failures in corporate accountability of maintaining a high standard of efficiency and probity in matters of remuneration, etc. Where failure to exercise such diligence was apparent, the regulator would request the institutional shareholders to come forward with a programme to remedy these defects forthwith. In cases where the intermediary investors had conspicuously failed in this respect, the regulator would have the power to 'name and shame'. It is for consideration whether there should also be the power to fine the investors, a matter which could be considered by the regulator in the first or a subsequent three-year review.

Achieving effective accountability

Such a system of regulation would not instantly rectify all the identified defects of accountability. But there is every chance that over time, and applied apolitically, the market forces of competition between investing institutions and the concern to avoid being 'named and shamed', as well as the provision of positive measures (the common obligation on all such investors to perform due diligence ensuring collective action), would bring about major improvements.

The simple obligation of due diligence in exercising voting rights is of far-reaching consequence. First, there would be the sanction of adverse publicity for investment institutions that failed to discharge their obligations. Second, the regulator could additionally recommend significant fines. Lastly, the institutions would be open to legal action by beneficiaries for any significant loss suffered as the result of continued negligence.

These actions, taken together, would go far effectively to enfranchise beneficial shareholders and eliminate the double accountability deficit, particularly when reinforced by the consequential reactions of markets.

Enfranchising individual shareholders

Before considering possible market reactions, one further matter needs brief consideration. The successful introduction of the reforms outlined would also bring substantial benefits to individual shareholders from overcoming the double accountability deficit and ensuring that companies are run in the general interests of all shareholders It is for consideration whether or not there should be any further specific reforms aimed at overcoming the essential powerlessness of individual shareholders (Chapter 2 and Figure 2, p. 5). There is a case for allowing all individual shareholders to elect one non-executive director of their own sole choosing. Their existing rights to vote on all director appointments could not be taken away – this would be an *additional* right. The directors concerned would have the same interests as all other directors to work in the interests of all shareholders. It is, however, a way of introducing a further independent non-executive for each company. If it were to be adopted it would cause existing bodies representing the interests of individual shareholders, such as the UK Shareholders Association (UKSA), to put forward suitable candidates.

The introduction of an additional individual shareholders' roll would represent a major step and one difficult to reverse. The prudent way forward is therefore for the Corporate Governance Regulator to consider the matter at the first three-year review, and invite all interested parties to put forward their views.

Possible market responses

The double accountability deficit can be remedied only by government initiative. The three proposed catalytic government actions as enshrined in the outline programme for reform would put investment institutions, fund managers, etc., under the clear legal obligation to hold corporate managements fully accountable to the interests of the ultimate shareholders. The institutions would have to respond to such obligations. How they would respond in these circumstances would be a matter for individual decisions and the effect of market forces in the changed legal circumstances.

The institutions, certainly the very large insurance companies, could be emboldened henceforth to act directly in the ultimate shareholders' interests on a continuous basis, as a few do now on an occasional selective basis. If they were seen to be able to discharge their new responsibilities effectively, other institutions could follow their example, including perhaps some of the large corporate pension funds. The same could apply to some of the large fund managers where the investment institutions delegated their governance obligations. For the majority of investment institutions, however, the continuing serious conflicts of interest would lead them to delegate their obligations to competent new specialist intermediaries which market forces would cause to emerge. In the interests of evaluating the efficacy of the proposed government actions some possible market responses are considered next. It must be stressed, however, that other and perhaps superior market responses could emerge. Indeed, as the investment institutions and regulators feel their way, it is likely that continually improving market responses would result.

Special Purpose Trust Companies

The most likely initial development to meet the needs of the majority

of investment institutions seeking to delegate their corporate governance obligations would be the emergence of a new form of investment
intermediary performing such services for a fee since no suitable entity
presently exists. Robert Monks has proposed just such a service
company (see Chapter 7) which he has termed a 'Special Purpose Trust
Company' (SPTC). These newly formed independent institutions' sole
function would be to act as owner, with full discretion with respect to
voting the shares held in the investment portfolios of its institutional
clients – i.e. to have full discretion to exercise independent judgement
in voting their clients' shares. To discharge this function they would
have to be completely independent institutions with no commercial
relationships with the companies to which their clients' shares related.
Staff would need a background in corporate governance and accountability. In practice, many would have a legal, accounting, financial or
business background. However, the staff would not be managing
businesses nor would they ever hold non-executive directorships. They
need corporate governance rather than business expertise.

The primary concern of SPTCs would be to create standards to guide
corporate managers and by which they would be judged. As they must
have no conflicts of interest, the best form of organization would be a
professional partnership, i.e. controlled and owned by their principals.
Further, senior staff should not be there only temporarily before
resuming a business career because of the obvious conflicts of interest.
Hence senior posts should be held only for the last, say, 5–10 years
before retirement.

SPTCs would be paid fees for their services to institutional clients,
determined competitively. The first responsibility of SPTCs would be
to monitor managements, vote on the appointments of all directors, and
ultimately vote to change boards when required. As long as the nomination committees of non-executive directors put forward competent
and independent candidates for non-executive director vacancies,
SPTCs would not need to find candidates themselves. But if in too
many companies unsuitable candidates were nominated, then the
SPTCs, acting collectively, would need to form organizations, supported by independent executive search firms, to find and recommend
suitable independent businesspeople as candidates. (Such candidates
would need to be predominantly businesspeople to carry the support of
corporate managements and direct and institutional shareholders.) The

second responsibility would be to provide guidance to managements on the long-term needs of owners, e.g. accountable long-term re-muneration incentives properly linked to performance, and requiring executive directors to share appropriately in investors' risks, perhaps by purchasing and *holding* a significant shareholding.

It is important to note that SPTCs would represent a *competitive market solution* to corporate governance needs. Their fees, and indeed their very existence, would depend on offering a valued commercial service in full competition with other providers.

The emergence of SPTCs in combination with the new corporate governance legal obligations and a regulator could well ensure sufficient accountability by both corporate managements and investment institutions such that no further developments would be needed. If, however, it became apparent that the combined direct action by some of the large institutions and SPTCs were unable to hold managements satisfactorily accountable, other types of institutions would be required, or might anyway emerge because of the extra benefits they could offer investment institutions in addition to taking over their legal obligation to act solely and exclusively in beneficiaries' interests.

Two forms of intermediaries might emerge, 'specialist investors' and 'relationship investors', both based on the benefits from small con-centrated specialist investment portfolios holding shares for the longer term and seeking board representation. To avoid any suggestion of possible monopoly power, the shares making up each intermediary's portfolio would be in a different industrial sector. The likely lengthen-ing of both long-term management incentives and fund management contracts – see below – would also favour the emergence of such investors. The model for such entities would be Warren Buffett's Berkshire-Hathaway company (see Chapters 2 and 6).

Specialist investors

'Specialist investors' (SIs) would in effect be specialist investment trusts aiming to hold 4–5 per cent shareholdings in perhaps only 5–10 com-panies. They would have small but experienced staffs made up of successful business executives and investment analysts. Their function would be select a very small number of companies for long-term investment and to be able and willing to act as supportive and knowledgeable long-term owners. In support of that activity they would seek board representation. (If competent, SPTCs and institutions would be likely to support their candidate directors. And, unlike SPTCs, the senior members of the SIs could and should be independent non-executive directors in the companies in which they invested, there being no conflicts of interests.) Their shareholders would be mainly the investment institutions, which would thus be relieved of corporate governance obligations in the underlying shares, although not for their shareholdings in the SIs. Such investor companies would offer investment institutions a potentially attractive way of securing the Berkshire-Hathaway type benefits of active, knowledgeable and committed share ownership in major companies. As with SPTCs, SIs would have to compete for business, hence they too would represent a competitive market solution for responsible share investment.

Relationship investors

The major investment institutions tend to hold investments in a large number of the top 200 companies for eight years or more on average, although they often trade actively in a part of such shareholdings. As no actual commitment to long-term holding is made, the Berkshire-Hathaway type advantages which accrue from an active, committed, stable relationship are foregone for investors and corporate managements alike. In addition to SIs, these advantages could be achieved by investment institutions and fund managers putting a proportion of their major company shareholdings into 'relationship investors' (RIs). Each RI would seek, on a very small portfolio of shares of perhaps 5–10 companies, to hold say 2 per cent of mega companies and up to 4–5 per cent of the rest of the top 100–200 companies, i.e. enough for influence but not dominance, typically holding shares for five years or more. They would each nominate suitable businessmen to be independent non-executive directors ('shareholder directors') voted on by all shareholders, and each backed up by a small secretariat to put them on equal terms with their executive colleagues. Their duties would be to *all* shareholders as now, but they would be providing fully independent and well supported director candidates who, if elected, would be able to count on the support of their RI. As most investment institutions and SPTCs, etc., would also tend to support them, they would be in a stronger position to hold corporate managements accountable. Equally, their knowledgeable support for approved longer-term management strategies would also be likely to result in widespread shareholder support, thus giving managements the confidence to undertake such strategies where passive absentee ownership and volatile share prices might otherwise make them too difficult or risky.

RIs and SIs could be paid a slightly enhanced, competitively deter-mined dividend *as decided by all shareholders* to cover their extra costs and responsibilities. This would be a market reward for the market service of providing ownership stability and truly independent non-executive directors on equal terms with executive directors and thus more able to hold them fully accountable. It would overcome the 'free-rider' problem and be to the clear benefit of all shareholders and ultimately all stakeholders. RIs could comprise both the larger investment institutions or syndicates of such institutions, probably organized by fund managers for a fee. It would not tie up institutionally held shares for any longer than at present, but an RI could always sell out before five years by forfeiting the enhanced dividends and another RI would take its place. It would be ideally suited to tracker funds with their very long-term holdings.

Both SIs and RIs could add to their effectiveness, on behalf of all shareholders, if their non-executive directors, in concert with any others, helped corporate managements in formulating their four- to five-year strategic plans. Such plans would form the basis of the longer-term incentive schemes for senior managers, a form of 'owner–management compact'. As SIs and RIs would be longer-term investors, their support, for as long as management performance justified it, would add to the confidence of managements and all other investors.

Longer fund management contracts

The final matter to be considered under possible market responses to changed corporate governance requirements concerns the length and security of fund management contracts. Most contracts run for five or six years, and some for much longer. But, as discussed earlier (Chapters 2 and 4), a fund manager would become concerned at the prospect of either dismissal or the loss of a large part of its investment fund responsibilities if its performance for a client, as measured quarterly, were not to be in the top median or quartile over the previous two or three years. Inevitably, this causes fund managers to favour shares expected to perform well on a short-term basis, which puts indirect but significant pressure on many corporate managements to pay more attention to short-term results. This, coupled with widely dispersed share portfolios, weakens investor support for otherwise justified longer-term corporate policies. The ultimate beneficial shareholders – primarily individuals saving for retirement – are of course investors who seek the best long-term returns. There are few incentives for fund managers to take as long-term a view as either their investment skills justify if only they could rely on longer-term loyalty from their clients, or as may be in the interests of beneficiaries. Yet it is widely acknowledged that investment performance measured over periods much shorter than five years (some would argue for a full economic cycle) are largely invalid. If, however, the investment institutions, in seeking the best performance for their beneficiaries, come to favour the Berkshire-Hathaway type benefits of more committed long-term ownership with the concomitant much smaller spread of shares which both SIs and RIs would provide, they should also consider the benefits from lengthened fund management contracts to an expected period of, say, five years, subject always to safeguards for interim performance. This would be welcomed by fund managers who would be freed to take longer-term views where justified. It would also complement the development of fiveyear long-term incentive schemes for corporate managements (presently more usually three years), and thus encourage longer-term corporate policies where desirable and justified.

There would be an important and welcome consequence of longer-term fund management contracts. The present pressures on most fund managers to become passive index funds (trackers) – now 25 per cent of the market, and rising – or their near cousins, 'closet indexers' (see Chapters 2 and 4), would abate. Fund managers could offer a far wider choice of risk and investment strategies which should be generally welcome. Furthermore, it would reduce the marked market volatility which results from copycat investment strategies.

Implications for the main participants

The proposed governance changes and likely market responses will have significant implications for all the main participants.

Non-executive directors

The major change for non-executives would be that they would no longer be chosen by their executive colleagues, but independently. Furthermore, they would have to be seen to act independently to retain their jobs. The starting position would be that the existing non-executives would comprise the whole of an independently advised board nomination committee. If they found truly independent and competent successors to propose to shareholders, the new arrangement might continue for some years. SPTCs, the first of the likely new investment intermediaries, would initially go along with their choices. But for companies that fail to put up appropriate non-executive candidates, or where performance of boards was unsatisfactory, SPTCs would collectively find and put up candidates of their own. Eventually, if RIs and SIs emerge – and this is likely because they would offer corporate managements knowledgeable long-term commitment and investors the prospects of better returns – these new intermediaries would be putting forward non-executive candidates of their own who would succeed if enough institutions, including SPTCs, supported them, again a likely development. In all these cases the candidates would continue to be experienced businesspeople, drawn from much the same people as now. But given the new mode of their appointments and the fact that their performance would be monitored (see proposed code of conduct above), a new experience for most, non-executive directors in future would be fully independent with no conflicts of interest. As the audit committee they alone would recommend auditors to shareholders. As the executive remuneration committee they would be independently advised and required to align senior management risk and rewards with those of shareholders. Finally, as the nomination committee, increasingly working with the newly emerging inter-mediaries, they would ensure independent successors.

Executive directors

The major change for executive directors would be that they would have to give up the powers assumed earlier when shareholders relinquished them. They would be freed to concentrate on their main priority – running the business – and be rewarded with appropriate longer-term incentives firmly linked to performance. Rewards could be as generous as now if truly earned. The alignment of their risks and rewards with shareholders would fully legitimisz them, and end the conflicts of interest, e.g. over takeovers and mergers, and remuneration. Competent managements would have nothing to fear and much to gain.

The investment institutions

The major change for the investment institutions would be that they would have to provide or procure the full discharge of the ownership responsibilities *solely* for the beneficiary shareholders, and in their *exclusive* interests. They would not want to run any risk of compromising their clear responsibilities to their beneficiaries by any perception of being beholden to corporate managements. This would mean, as the conflict of interest would remain, that most of them would want to delegate their fiduciary responsibilities to the newly emerging intermediaries. First and foremost, they would choose the SPTCs, but increasingly also the RIs and SIs with their prospects of better long-term performance for beneficiaries. Only the largest insurance companies, and a handful of the very largest pension funds, would be likely to choose to act directly. Pension fund trustees could no longer divide their loyalty between their corporate managements and their members on corporate governance matters. Nor could they continue to be largely passive. Increasingly trustees would be elected mainly by their members and even solely where defined contribution schemes displace defined benefit schemes. Trustees would have much increased responsibilities, would need to be better trained, and would deserve appropriate fees (see also the Myners Report – Chapter 7).

Fund managers

A major change would occur for fund managers. The pension fund trustees and other fiduciaries would be required to provide or procure the discharge of their ownership responsibilities having regard solely and exclusively to their beneficiaries' interests by either

1. discharging the responsibility directly (rare save for the largest insurance companies and pension funds); or
2. delegating it explicitly to fund managers; or
3. delegating it directly to newly formed specialist intermediaries, such as SPTCs.

Choices (1) and (3) would remove a potentially onerous liability from fund managers, and would free them to concentrate on their main expertise of investment. Choice (2) could be accepted by fund managers with an SPTC level fee – or delegated to a SPTC. The fund managers' days of either trying vainly to discharge onerous corporate governance responsibilities without the incentive or means, or of avoiding them altogether, would be over.

Consultants and auditors

Major changes would occur for consultants and auditors. Executive remuneration consultants would need to choose whether to advise corporate managements on management and employee schemes, or remuneration committees on executive director remuneration, for they could no longer do both. The same would apply to executive search firms. Finally, accounting firms would have to provide a client company either with audit services or consultancy services, a trend already apparent. These changes would avoid the disabling conflicts of interest for all concerned. There would be no overall loss of business, merely a rearrangement of clients.

An evaluation of the proposed changes

The final task is to evaluate the proposed changes and the likely market responses to them from the viewpoint of the main players.

Beneficiaries

The prime weakness of contemporary corporate governance is absentee ownership caused by the double accountability deficit. The interests of shareholders, individual and beneficial, suffer alike from their essential powerlessness. They need countervailing powers to ensure their interests are given the primacy they deserve. The proposed changes (and in particular the requirement for trustees, etc., to act solely and exclusively in beneficiaries' interests) and the likely market responses should together restore the balance in their favour.

Government

A sensible guideline when considering the case for government involvement in the economic sphere is the old adage 'the market where possible, the government where necessary'. In recent years, governments have come under increasing pressure to intervene in corporate governance matters, e.g. legislate on senior management remuneration and takeovers. These calls are usually based on a wrong analysis. There is a strong case for some government involvement, but it should be limited to the relatively modest catalytic actions outlined, including a corporate governance regulator with a light touch. Market forces would then be freed by the elimination of the present entrenched conflicts of interest to do the rest. With trustees, etc., having to work solely and exclusively for beneficiaries, independent non-executive directors would be able to hold corporate managements accountable, with their remuneration firmly tied to long-term performance. This would be far superior to legislation requiring specified shareholder approval at AGMs. Further, even mega companies would start to become accountable. The proposed actions would thus resolve the main governance issues which have concerned governments.

Boards of directors

Overcoming public disquiet By freeing both executives and non-executive directors to concentrate on their separate functions, boards of directors would be much more effective. They would be largely freed from persistent public criticism because the main causes of such criticisms would have been removed. Executive remuneration would be independently determined on appropriate criteria. Takeovers and mergers would continue, but with fully independent non-executive directors would have to promise clear benefits to all shareholders. Further, the persistent clamour for either European style two-tier boards, or the American system of mainly non-executive boards, both alien to UK corporate culture, would be stilled. The reforms would obviate the need for them.

Creating divisive boards? It might be argued that having fully independent non-executive directors would be divisive and, by implication, damage corporate performance. The argument cannot be sustained. First, all directors have an overriding duty to shareholders which the proposed changes strongly reinforce. Second, it is untrue and naïve to pretend that the interests of owners and management always coincide. Manifestly they do not (e.g. over management remuneration, acquisition and disposals, takeover defences, and management buy-outs). The proposals reflect this reality and provide an effective mechanism for reconciling differences by harmonising the main long-term interests of both parties, while providing the means and incentives for superior long-term performance. Further, they could be expected to attract the highest calibre directors of both types because they would give them the chance to exercise their complementary talents to the full. Finally, companies with fully independent directors would attract stronger market support for their corporate strategies.

Directors' remuneration

Executive directors Instead of stock options being the main form of senior management remuneration, the remuneration committees would want the non-guaranteed form of reward to be one that directly aligns the longer-term risks and rewards of managements and investors. One of the best ways would be to have the reward in two parts. First, senior managements would be required to invest up to a year's salary in their companies' shares *to be held for the longer of the agreed incentive period or while they remained in employment* – this being the price for participating in a well-incentivized scheme. Second, the main reward should be to award shares generously for meeting a typically four- to five-year stretching business plan. If paid partly or mainly in shares, as would be desirable, there should be further incentives to continue to hold them. This general approach is in the best long-term interests of shareholders, and with appropriately generous incentives should appeal to competent managers.

Non-executives   The remuneration non-executives needs to reflect that the proposals would put added burdens on these directors. The job would require more time and commitment – perhaps double the present typical 12–15 days. Few people of the right calibre would have the time or energy for more than two such appointments, and many might manage only one. The second consideration is whether fees should be cash, shares (to be held during the term of employment) or a mixture. A mixture seems preferable as it would combine sufficient long-term incentives without the risk of becoming overcommitted to managements' longer-term plans if circumstances later require changes.

Sufficient non-executive candidates?   The candidates for fully independent non-executive directors would be most likely to come from the same pool as now. The job would be much more satisfying, have strong shareholder support, confer unquestioned independent status and be better paid, leading to ample qualified candidates. While performance would be monitored, that should not discourage competent people.

Investment institutions

The proposals should have a strong attraction to investment institutions, which would be released from their present disabling conflicts of interest and the concomitant and growing media, public and political criticisms of their actions (or inactions). They should also result in better performance. The institutions would have to be more effective in their trustee and fiduciary roles, but would have the necessary means and incentives.

Fund managers

The trustees and fiduciaries of the investment institutions, in the interests of their beneficiaries to whom they would now be effectively accountable, would be likely to encourage longer-term fund management contracts – see above. Fund managers would then be able to demonstrate their investment skills more satisfactorily. The pressures for most to become trackers or 'closet indexers' would abate. Tracker funds, which historically have played little part in corporate governance, would need to change or delegate to SPTCs.

There would also be valuable new fee-earning opportunities for fund managers to organize syndicated RIs and SIs to which their skills are well suited. Tracker funds, with their very long-term commitment to companies (i.e. for as long as they are in a particular index), would have a particular incentive for these roles.

Shareholder activist funds

These funds, with their impressive performance in effecting beneficial changes in underperforming companies and earning a superior return for their investors, would be in more demand than ever. The investment institutions would no longer be inhibited from investing in them for fear of upsetting corporate managements, and indeed should welcome more of them.

Employees and other stakeholders

Both employees and other stakeholders would benefit from the proposed changes. Companies would have every chance of raising their longer-term performance since the interests of direct and beneficial shareholders would prevail, which is in the clear and general long-term interest of all the other participants in the corporate process (Chapter 6).

Private equity firms

The proposed changes would have some effect on the private equity (venture capital firms). With improved incentives for quoted corporate performance, there would be less need to take companies private to realize their longer-term potential.

The potential outcome

The proposed catalytic government actions would cause major and permanent changes in British corporate governance. The intentions of the traditional long-hallowed governance system, whereby corporate managements were fully accountable to shareholders, and their interests aligned (Figure 1, p. 2), would be restored. The breakdown of the traditional model, which has led to the present reality whereby shareholders have largely relinquished their powers, with most of them plus some additional ones centred on executive directors (Figure 2, p. 5), would be overcome. Powers would be exercised by the investment institutions in combination with new investment intermediaries solely and exclusively on behalf of beneficial shareholders. Some investment institutions, almost certainly a small minority, would choose to discharge their obligations by direct action, with the majority seeking to delegate to specialist intermediaries. The types of intermediaries would depend on the market response, but three possible and complementary responses – SPTCs, SIs and RIs – have been considered. Other and perhaps superior ones could well evolve.

In the first instance, as the investment institutions and the regulator would be feeling their way, the SPTC response would be likely to predominate, and this is illustrated in Figure 3 (p. 19). (In the interests of simplicity, Figure 3 shows only SPTCs. But if SIs and RIs came to pass the SPTC box could be expanded to include them for the control lines would be essentially the same.) The reforms, assisted by a corporate governance regulator, would put shareholder interests in a dominant position. All the investment institutions and new intermediaries would have that as an obligation. It is conceivable that if SPTCs were to be fully effective in holding corporate managements accountable, then other types of intermediaries might not be needed, at least at first. The clear benefits to corporate managements and shareholders of active, knowledgeable and committed ownership of the Berkshire-Hathaway type, however, would be likely to lead to SIs and RIs and similar developments – the market would decide. But by various means the proposed reforms would ensure that all institutionally held shares (up to 80 per cent) would be voted solely and exclusively in beneficiaries' interests, mainly by SPTCs, and that by holding managements truly accountable, all the present major corporate governance weaknesses and conflicts of interest would be overcome. (If eventually individual shareholders had the right to elect one non-executive director, this would widen direct accountability to all shareholders.) The necessary incentives, to ensure that shareholder votes would be used on a continuously effective basis on behalf of the real shareholders, would be firmly in place. Managements would be relieved of their present necessarily assumed but inappropriate non-management powers, which properly belong to shareholders. They would be freed from the present rising tide of serious and largely justified criticisms, which in any case cannot be ignored much longer. They would then be able to concentrate on corporate performance, their prime responsibility. Finally, managements would have both fully legitimized, generous incentives and the preconditions for long-term performance to the direct benefit of beneficiary investors and individual shareholders, and to the indirect but general benefit of all stakeholders. The enhanced longer-term profitability from all corporate decisions being taken essentially in shareholders' interests would considerably outweigh the modest costs of implementation. In sum, all involved would benefit, and all could play to their long-term strengths relieved of conflicts of interest and other handicaps.

CHAPTER 9

Capitalism for Tomorrow

This final chapter puts the proposals for overcoming the corporate governance weaknesses in a wider perspective. First, the justification for good governance is considered from a national viewpoint. Second, the benefits of reform are evaluated against the costs. Third, is an explanation of why reforms have been so difficult to achieve, and why some government involvement is inescapable. Fourth, is the justification for adding somewhat to an already formidable financial regulatory burden. Finally, and most importantly, the crucial contribution of free markets to improved corporate governance is set out.

The wider justification for good corporate governance

Corporate governance should not be narrowly viewed as a subject mainly confined to directors, investment institutions and fund managers. Corporations are very powerful in modern society. With the worldwide tendency for mergers and acquisitions, many of which lead to global mega companies, that power is increasing to the point where even governments go in awe of such companies. Yet at present power is concentrated in the hands of self-perpetuating corporate boards, particularly executive directors (Figure 2). There is little effective accountability to shareholders or anyone else. Such a concentration of unaccountable power is unhealthy and, in democratic societies, ultimately unsustainable. It inevitably leads to abuses, of which the often huge senior management rewards poorly related to performance is the most prominent. Too many modern corporations are viewed as the creature of their senior managers whose interests predominate. It is a main cause of the major decline in business popularity over the last thirty years despite unprecedented economic success. This should be a matter of concern across the political spectrum (Chapter 1).

Society gives business its licence to operate and its many privileges such as limited liability. Business conduct must be seen to be in harmony with society's values or changes will be imposed. Already there is growing agitation on ethics, over health and environmental damage, over poorly paid foreign workers particularly if they are children, etc., leading to product boycotts and calls for restrictive legislation. The best-run corporations are responding to these pressures as the growing membership of household name companies in the Institute of Business Ethics (1986), the Centre for Tomorrow's Company (1996), etc., bear witness. There is, however, the clear evidence that well-governed companies work in the best interests of society in general as well as for all who are directly involved (Chapter 6). This insight underlay Robert Monks's well-argued views that there should be no corporate power without accountability (Chapter 7), a view that I strongly endorsed in my own proposals for modest but essential government action (Chapter 8).

There is a justified and growing acceptance that the wider public has a legitimate interest in good corporate governance. Jonathan Charkham in *Keeping Good Company* put the point well:

> The corporate governance system is as important to a nation as any other crucial part of its institutional framework, because on it depends a good portion of the nation's prosperity. It contributes to social cohesion in a way too little recognised. A proper framework for the exercise of power is an economic necessity, a political requirement and a moral imperative.

The same view informed Robert Monks's and Nell Minow's definition of healthy corporate governance as 'the relationship among various participants in determining the direction and performance of corporations *consistent with the public good*'.[1] The Hampel Report (Chapter 7) commended the same general view. It strongly endorsed shareholder primacy but recognized it could be pursued objectively only by developing and sustaining stakeholder objectives. Crucially, it stated that companies should have regard to the broader public acceptability of their conduct.

It is these legitimate wider public concerns over the health of corporate governance that justify the interest of political parties. Ultimately, corporations can flourish only in cohesive communities and, where necessary, with the involvement of governments.

Costs vs. benefits

Most of the official corporate governance investigations (Chapter 7) endorsed the clear benefits from good corporate governance, and none more so than the Hampel Report. It stated that sound corporate governance has a neglected contribution to make to national efficiency and prosperity. These gains would arise in a fully reformed system (e.g. from implementing the proposals of Chapter 8, which of course go far beyond anything contemplated in the Hampel Report) primarily from three related changes. First would be the realignment of corporate managements' risks and rewards with those of their underlying investors on a longer-term basis (a major Greenbury Report recom-mendation), i.e. clearly linking incentives to long-term performance and avoiding poor value takeovers and mergers, etc. Second, this process would be strongly reinforced by extending fund management contracts, with due safeguards, typically to a five-year basis. Third, there is the strong evidence that well-governed companies are worth significantly more, and further would be the clear beneficiaries from appropriately motivating and valuing their stakeholders (Chapter 6).

The gains would thus be very considerable. There would be extra costs involved to achieve these gains. The investment institutions and fund managers would have to give time and money to the active discharge of ownership responsibilities solely and exclusively in their beneficiaries' interests, or more probably pay SPTCs and other likely new investment intermediaries to do it for them. These fees would, however, be competitively determined. Such fees, plus any direct costs, would be modest in relation to the clear potential gains, hence the overall cost–benefit ratio would strongly favour the case for good governance.

The barriers to acceptable accountability

British corporate governance presently fails the acid test of any governance system that those to whom major powers are entrusted must be accountable to those whom they serve. Stewards, deprived of effective accountability for long periods, the present reality, will normally pursue self-interest to a greater or lesser degree. Such accountability as does exist at present (Figure 2) is typically limited and delayed. This will persist until the resultant absentee ownership can be overcome. The intermediaries must become effectively accountable to their beneficiaries, and corporate managements to the intermediaries.

The only question is how accountability can be accomplished. Its achievement has been shown to be in the clear long-term interests of all the main participants. This even applies to senior managements, despite their many present powers, because market concerns and growing public and political disquiet mean that change is inevitable. The best managements know this, and indeed would welcome the legitimization of their rewards in the more attractive conditions permitting raised corporate performances which superior governance would provide.

The fact that all, or certainly nearly all, of the participants would benefit from the introduction of full accountability and superior governance, however, in no way ensures this will come to pass. The prime reason is the one identified by the multidisciplined American economist, Mancur Olson, in his seminal book.[2] He showed that unless the members of a group were few, or unless there were coercion or some other special device, that they could not and would not act to achieve their common or group interest. This arises because there needs to be a sufficient incentive for enough of the individuals to act together, to make the necessary effort and to bear the costs, even though, if successful, all the non-contributing members will benefit at no cost (i.e. overcoming the 'free-rider' problem). Applying this insight to the investment institutions, it is clear that none have a sufficient individual incentive since all are the victim of conflicts of interest. The risks of acting alone would be unacceptable. This applies particularly to the competing fund managers, for if only one or two took the lead and offended corporate managements, they could lose the greater part of their occupational pension fund business. Finally, it applies with even more force to the millions of individual shareholders and the 15 million or so ultimate beneficiaries, the real shareholders. This illustrates the fundamental difference in how ineffectively self-interested large groups will behave compared with small ones.

In the case of corporate governance, the position could hardly be less favourable to collective action. There is not just one large group that needs to act but several, each with little contact with the others, and in the case of the real shareholders, none at all. It is this that explains why, despite the many worthy attempts at reform in the 1990s, little real change was effected. The groups' inertias were impossible to overcome, especially by what were essentially appeals for more enlightened behaviour, without effective sanctions. Effective action requires effective countervailing power.

The systemic fault that so handicaps contemporary British corporate governance is not the fault of any of the main participants. Nor can any of them procure the remedy. The only conceivable catalyst for beneficial change, for providing effective countervailing power, is enlightened government action. If that is rejected, very little progress in a vital but neglected area of national life is possible.

The proposed extension of regulation, correctly viewed, is therefore fully justified. It is to ensure that shareholder rights are actively, efficiently and continuously discharged solely and exclusively on behalf of their beneficial owners. This is self-evidently desirable and occurs too infrequently under present arrangements.

Regulatory overburden

British business in general is suffering from an excess of regulation which grows by the year. The City in particular suffers even more. The very wide powers of the main regulator, the Financial Services Authority, make the financial sector in Britain the most heavily regulated in the world. It receives more regulation than the powerful Securities and Exchange Commission, hitherto the world trend-setter, imposes on Wall Street. Therefore the imposition of even the proposed light regulation for corporate governance may be unwelcome. The answer, however, is not to reject the further proposed governance regulation as a step too far. The prospective gains for all concerned should far outweigh the modest costs involved. Reform is also essential to the guardianship of the majority of people's main assets on which their living standards in retirement largely depend. The right course is rather to trim back other financial regulations where the costs outweigh the benefits, the exact opposite situation to governance reform.

The contribution of free markets

While the systemic corporate governance weakness is seen to be against the long-term interest of all the main governance participants, none of them have either the individual or collective ability to put matters right. Nor can free market mechanisms overcome the disincentives and conflicts of interest despite the major prospective all round gains, or it would have happened. Only government intervention, the relatively modest proposed catalytic government actions, can overcome the constraints to beneficial change. But once enacted, free-market forces would come into their own. They would give rise to the most appropriate new forms of investment intermediaries capable of overcoming all the conflicts of interests efficiently.

There is a very strong likelihood of something like SPTCs developing quickly. This would probably be followed by longer-term investors of different kinds, such as SIs and RIs. These would provide the significant advantages that *owners* could offer to the investment institutions and fund managers who would be under the requirement to work solely and exclusively in the interests of the ultimate beneficiaries. Other and perhaps superior investment intermediaries could well arise under the effect of competitive markets. But in whatever form efficient new intermediaries emerged, the investment institutions and their fund managers would be freed from the constraints of the present serious conflicts of interest. They could concentrate on their prime function of efficient and probably longer-term investment in their clients' best interests. Thus the proposed reforms would enable competitive free-market forces to perform their prime function, the efficient allocation of resources. As Robert Monks well expressed it, 'Putting owners in charge of what they own is the purest form of capitalism.'

Notes

Introduction

1. Stanley Wright, *Two Cheers for the Institutions*, Social Market Foundations, Paper No. 19, 1994.

Executive Summary

1. This is one of the main issues being considered over the period 1999-2000 by the DTI Company Law Review Steering Group on Modern Company Law for a Competitive Economy.

Chapter 1

1. Kevin Brown, 'Approval of big business in Britain at 30-year low', *The Financial Times*, 22 February 1999.
2. John Plender, *A Stake in the Future*, Nicholas Brearly Publishing, 1997.
3. Rupert Pennant-Rea, 'A survey of capitalism – punters or proprietors?', *The Economist*, 5 May 1990.
4. *Developing a Winning Partnership – How companies and institutional investors are working together*, revised edition, published by the DTI, September 1996, also widely known as the Myners Report. This report is discussed in Chapter 7.
5. *The Millennium Book: A Century of Investment Returns*, a joint study by the London Business School and ABN Amro, February 2000.
6. Philip Coggan, 'A smaller share', *The Financial Times,* 22 December 1999.
7. Letter from Investors Relations Society Chairman, *The Financial Times,* 1 May 1998.
8. *Fund Management of City Business Services 1997*, a publication by British INVISIBLES and also the PDFM publication cited in Table 1.3 above.
9. *Fund Management Survey 1999*, for the Institutional Fund Managers Association, October 1999.
10. *Investment Strategy for Pension Funds*, Schroders, June 1998.
11. A 1990 survey of 1,600 pension funds by the performance measurement specialist WM found that nearly two-thirds of the 300 funds which had switched fund managers since January 1998 had switched from a wide discretionary approach to a

specialized one where the manager invests in an agreed, specified asset type. But the new customized portfolios were being managed in very similar ways to the old ones in terms of asset allocation. This switch has cost an estimated 2 per cent of portfolio value merely for similar assets and similar performance (Jane Martinson, 'Pension funds seek specialisation', *The Financial Times,* 7 October 1998).

12. 'Boardroom pay – creamed', *The Economist,* 27 November 1999.
13. 'Directors' pay report 1999', by Income Data services, see Robert Taylor's article, *The Financial Times,* 28 October 1999.
14. Tony Jackson, 'The fat cats keep getting fatter', *The Financial Times,* 1 August 1998.
15. Ruth Lea, 'Directors' remuneration', IoD Research Paper, March 1997.
16. A. P. Williams, *Just reward? – the truth about top executive pay,* Kogan Page, 1994.
17. John W. Hunt, 'Profits, pay and teamwork', *The Financial Times,* 15 July 1995.
18. Paola Bradley, Chris Hendry and Stephen Perkins, 'Is there a market for top pay?', *Corporate Governance Newsletter,* May 1997.

Chapter 2

1. 'Non-executive directors – watchdogs or advisors', by City Research Association Ltd., for BDO Binder Hamlyn, July 1994 – a survey of executive and non-executive directors and their main advisers.
2. Jane Martinson, 'Shares in action', *The Financial Times,* 27 April 1998.
3. *Social Trends, 1999* – latest figures 1997.
4. Jane Martinson, 'Pension funds do better when they retain managers', *The Financial Times,* 19 October 1998.
5. Adrian Michaels and Michael Peel, 'PWC nears ground-breaking split' and 'PWC is counting on technological change', *The Financial Times,* 18 February 2000.
6. 'Boards lack a sense of venture', City Editor Commentary, *The Times,* 15 May 1998.
7. See Richard Waters, 'CEO pay soars as the mergers multiply', *The Financial Times,* 25 March 1999. The evidence presented for America applies equally to Britain.
8. In America, similar unsatisfactory accounting rules prevail, but options are typically huge, both for individual senior managers, especially the CEOs, and in relation to corporate profits. There are also large numbers of employee stock options. See Philip Coggan, 'US profits overstated by a third, says report', *The Financial Times,* 17b April 1998. The article was based on an April 1998 report, No. 17 by Smithers & Co., a London-based investment research firm. It is estimated that profits in the top 100 American companies should have been 30 per cent lower than reported in 1995 and 36 per cent lower in 1996, such that a number of major household names would have reported losses if stock option costs had been properly disclosed. Similar numbers still apply.
9. Joel Stern, 'Boost [directors'] performance by removing caps on pay', *The Sunday Times,* 9 January 2000.
10. The conforming with 'best practice' will always leave out superior new ideas. It is a flawed standard.
11. Even Warren Buffett and BH cannot be successful every year, and the day may come when it should perhaps be broken up. This is the theme of a recent article – John Jay, 'Time for Buffett to break up Berkshire Hathaway', *The Sunday Times,* 9 January 2000. Jay points out that BH has underperformed the 'Standard and Poors 500' index

by 31 per cent during 1999 (since partly recovered), and accordingly should now be broken up. He may be right but Buffett is unlikely to take such a decision on the evidence of one year's poor results. Few will be too surprised if BH recovers.

Chapter 3

1. The word 'hostile' is mainly used by a defending company's board to describe an unwelcome bid.
2. Graham Serjeant, 'UK must play fantasy global league', *The Times,* 7 January 1999.
3. See for example: Andy Cosh, Alan Hughes and Ajit Singh, *Takeovers and Short-Termism in the UK*, Institute for Public Policy Research, 1999; Matthew Bishop, 'A survey of corporate governance, *The Economist*, 29 January 1994; 'Why too many mergers miss the mark', *The Economist*, 4 January 1997; Neil Monnery and Robert Malchione, 'Seven deadly sins of mergers' *The Financial Times*, 2 March 2000.
4. 'How to make mergers work', and 'How to merge – after the deal', *The Economist*, 9 January 1999.
5. Lawrence Capron, 'Making mergers pay off', *Impact*, University of Western Ontario, August 1998.
6. 'Mergers & acquisitions – unlocking shareholder value: the keys to success', KPMG Global Research Report, November 1999.
7. David Pilling, 'Making its Merck on its own', *The Financial Times*, 4 February 2000.
8. 'Drug-induced seizures', *The Economist*, 13 November 1999.
9. Tony Jackson, 'Drug giants that are much too addicted to mergers', *The Financial Times*, 16 November 1999.
10. 'A view from the ground', Editorial, *The Financial Times,* 12 February 2000.
11. Andrew Hill, 'Let the buyer beware', *The Financial Times*, 27 October 1999.

Chapter 4

1. American turnover is now much higher. On average every share of every company on the New York Stock Exchange changes hands at the rate of once a year compared with once every three years in 1981, and every six years in 1974 – see 'Wake-up call', *The Economist*, 25 March 2000.
2. 'PDFM pension fund indicators – a long term perspective on pension fund investment – 1998' and the Final Report of the Hampel Committee on Corporate Governance, January 1998.
3. Letter from Investors Relations Society Chairman, *The Financial Times*, 1 May 1998.
4. Barry Riley, 'Short-termism revisited and recalculated', *The Financial Times*, 16 April 1997.
5. Ian Orton, 'Churn – just why are portfolios turned over so often?', *The Financial Times*, 16/17 October 1999.
6. Simon Targett, 'Fund managers dubbed incompetent lemmings', *The Financial Times,* 25 February 2000.
7. Christopher Fildes, 'How do you run a big pension fund? Start with a small one and think for yourself', *Spectator*, 27 February 1999.

Chapter 5

1. Dido Sandler, 'Alternatives to pensions – more than one way to finance retirement', *The Financial Times*, 5 February 2000.
2. Simon English, 'Personal pensions are the pits', *Sunday Telegraph*, 13 June 1999.
3. Anne Ashworth (*The Times* Personal Finance Editor), 'Pensions', *The Times*, 30 June 1999.
4. Sandy Leitch, 'After mis-selling, the clean-up', Personal View Column, *The Financial Times*, 9 December 1999.
5. Graham Serjeant, 'Crash puts stake in stakeholder plan', *The Times,* 29 October 1998.
6. 'The end of the company pension – passing the buck', *The Economist'*, 15 May 1999.
7. Barry Riley, 'End of a golden age', *The Financial Times*, 25/26 March 2000.

Chapter 6

1. This is one of the main issues being considered over the period 1999–2000 by the DTI Company Law Review Steering Group on Modern Company Law for a Competitive Economy. The Steering Group's recommendations could well lead to significant changes in company law.
2. Graham Serjeant, 'Shareholders are still the best guardians of success', *The Times*, 2 January 1997.
3. Graham Serjeant, 'The ambivalent face of capitalism', *The Times*, 8 April, 1999.
4. A brief analysis of the views of some leading stakeholder advocates is set out in the next chapter.
5. Jacques Bughin and Thomas Z. Copeland, 'The virtuous circle of shareholder value creation', *McKinsey Quarterly,'* 1997, No. 2.
6. 'Employment Performance', The McKinsey Global Institute, November 1994.
7. Mike Phillips, Philip Sadler and Daniel Edington, 'The inclusive approach and business success – the research evidence', an interim report by the Centre for Tomorrow's Company, November 1997. The Centre is a policy institute formed in 1996 to encourage British businessmen to increase their profits by considering all their relationships with their employees, customers, suppliers and communities, as well as shareholders, as primary relationships. It demonstrated that what it has termed the 'inclusive approach' is in the best interests of shareholders and all the other listed groups. It advocates that company managements should value all their primary relationships not just those of shareholders, but it sees the relationship as being responsible for and not to the other key groups.
8. Arie de Geus, *The Living Company – Growth, Learning and Longevity in Business,* Nicholas Brearley Publishing, 1997. The author worked for Royal Dutch Shell in three continents over thirty-eight years to the end 1980s, and is the originator of the concept of 'the learning organization'. See also Tony Jackson's book review for *The Financial Times*, 15 May 1997.
9. R. Maitland, *Employee Morale in the High Performance Organisations*, International Survey Research Ltd., 1994.
10. Frederick F Reichheld, *The Loyalty Effect: the Hidden Force behind Growth Profits and*

Lasting Value, Harvard Business School Press, 1996. See also Richard Donkin's review article, 'The age of the one-night stand', *The Financial Times,* 12 April 1996.

11. See William Lewis, 'Governance and share price linked says new analysis', *The Financial Times,* 17 May 1997.

12. R. LaPorta, F. Lopez-de-Silanes, A. Schleifer and R. Vishny, 'Investor protection and corporate value', NBER Working Paper 7403. See also 'Protection money', *The Economist*, 11 December 1999.

13. Roland F. Felton, Alex Hudnut and Jennifer van Heeckeren, 'Putting a value on board governance, *McKinsey Quarterly*, 1996, No. 4.

Chapter 7

1. Jonathan Charkham, *Keeping Good Company – A Study of Corporate Governance in Five Countries*, Clarendon Press, 1994.
2. Jonathan Charkham and Anne Simpson, *Fair Shares – The Future of Shareholder Power and Responsibility*, Oxford University Press, 1999.
3. John Plender, *A Stake in the Future*, Nicholas Brearly Publishing, 1997.
4. 'Thank you and goodbye – bad bosses in big companies in America are more at risk these days than ever before', *The Economist*, 3 October 1998.
5. Charles Elson, 'Shareholding non-executives should limit excessive directors' pay', *The Financial Times,* 28 July 1995.
6. Will Hutton, *The State We're In*, Jonathan Cape, 1995.
7. See (i) *The State to Come*, Vintage Books, 1997; and (ii) 'Stakeholding and its critics', IEA Health and Welfare Unit, 1997, No. 36.
8. John Kay and Aubrey Silberston, 'Corporate governance', *National Institute Economic Review*, August 1995.
9. *The Financial Times*, 22 August 1995.
10. John Kay, 'The capitalist conscience', *The Financial Times,* 27 February 1999.
11. Robert Monks, *The Emperor's Nightingale – Restoring the Integrity of the Corporation,* Capstone, 1998.

Chapter 8

1. Patience Wheatcroft, 'Please don't rock the boat – I'm a non-executive director', *The Times*, 14 March 2000.
2. My debt to the insights and analysis of Robert Monks – see previous chapter – on the first two requirements and the discussion of SPTCs in the next section is fully acknowledged.

Chapter 9

1. Robert A. G. Monks and Nell Minow, *Corporate Governance,* Blackwell, 1995.
2. Mancur Olson, *The Logic of Collective Action,* Harvard University Press, 1965 and 1971.

Index